ENERGIZING ENTREPRENEURS

Charting a Course for Rural Communities

by Deborah Markley

Don Macke

Vicki B. Luther

e²

Book Design: Reynold Peterson

Published by the Heartland Center for Leadership Development

Printed in the United States of America

ISBN 0-9747027-2-2

PREFACE

Energizing Entrepreneurs: Charting a Course for Rural Communities
has arrived on the scene at a critical time for communities
throughout rural America. Rural communities are beginning to
rethink the premises upon which their economic development
strategies are based. They are reassessing their economic opportunities and redefining themselves. They are building on their
assets and their entrepreneurial capacity. Community leaders are
embracing new economic development models that emphasize
entrepreneurship.

Rural communities cannot undertake this transformative journey alone. Communities provide the immediate environment in
which entrepreneurs can flourish, but they need tools and
resources to identify and build upon assets, make choices, learn
and innovate. This guide should become a well-worn map for
community leaders as they chart their course for energizing
entrepreneurs.

But, communities also need partners, making regional cooperation critically important. Entrepreneurs need access to all the
resources available within their regions. Political jurisdictions
have no economic rationale and few rural communities have the
resources to match opportunity with need. Community leaders
need to reach across political and geographic boundaries to partner with others who are committed to building an entrepreneurial rural America.

From my national vantage point, I see a new rural
entrepreneurial culture and climate flourishing across the country.
In those places where this new culture is becoming deeply root-

ed, three principles apply. It is entrepreneur focused. It is strongly based in communities. It is regionally oriented to reach scale and expand capacity. These same principles apply to the knowledge, stories and tools shared in the pages that follow. I hope you'll embrace them in the work you do in your communities.

Finally, the need for enhanced understanding of how entrepreneurship development strategies contribute to the creation of sustainable rural economies is great. We need to learn from your work in the field and to share this knowledge with policy makers at the state and federal levels. RUPRI is committed to doing the research and facilitating a dialogue about how public policy can support your efforts to energize an entrepreneurial rural America. I look forward to joining you in these efforts.

Chuck Fluharty
Director, Rural Policy Research Institute

ACKNOWLEDGEMENTS

As with all great endeavors, this book has been a collaborative undertaking. The authors worked together to bring the best insights of their respective organizations to each chapter in this guide. We value and appreciate the input of our colleagues in the RUPRI Center for Rural Entrepreneurship–Brian Dabson and Craig Schroeder. Many of the stories we share in this book were originally developed by Lisa Bauer, "Entrepreneur of the Month" Editor for the RUPRI Center, and we greatly appreciate her ability to bring these entrepreneurs to life on the page. We benefited from the editing of Milan Wall with assistance from Reggi Carlson. As always, Taina Radenslaben's cheerful support in helping us keep both the book and website development on track is gratefully acknowledged. Graphic designer Reynold Peterson and web designer Jean Bourdreau, helped translate our vision for the book and companion website into a reality that is both visually appealing and, we hope, easy for you to use.

We appreciate the insights that a group of practitioners shared with us in the early stages of preparing this guide: Katherine Baril, Don Betts, Mark Burdette, Burt Chojnowski, Greg Clary, Brian Dabson, Chris Gibbons, June Holley, Ron Hustedde, Wally Kearns, Kathy Moxon, Tom Lyons, Erik Pages, Craig Schroeder, Leslie Scott, and Dennis West. This group of early innovators in the field of entrepreneurship development has been a source of inspiration and support to us as we have deepened our understanding of this work.

Most importantly, this book reflects what we have learned from countless community economic development practitioners who wake up each day asking what they can do to energize the entrepreneurs in their particular rural places and who are helping create more entrepreneurial rural communities. Your work has made it possible for us to create this roadmap to help other rural community leaders chart an entrepreneurial course for their communities. We commend your efforts, we value what we've learned from you and we will continue to support your work through our Centers' activities.

Deb Markley
Don Macke
Vicki Luther

CONTENTS

CHAPTER 1
CHARTING YOUR
OWN COURSE

There are about 600,000 places you can go to on the Internet to explore "rural entrepreneurship." It's quite a journey. We know. As the authors of this book, we have been to many of those places—in person! We have worked with hundreds of people whose stories make up the mounting number of case studies on rural entrepreneurship. And we have collaborated with dozens of scholars and specialists who are documenting, disseminating and just plain figuring out why entrepreneurship promises to be an important economic engine for rural places in the 21st century.

Our guess is that you don't have time right now to take a long journey. That is why we have written this book. Our goal is to help you help your community to chart its own course toward an entrepreneurial future. We will provide you with the best tools we know of to help you find your way. We will suggest a few short-cuts. We will warn you about detours that can eat up your scarce resources of time and money. And we will help you bring others on board, so you're not out there all alone, trying to do everything yourself.

Our Audience

If you happen to be a person with a great idea for a new venture that could really take off—if you could just learn a little bit more about marketing—this book is not for you. Pass this book on to the person in your rural community who is helping you get financial assistance, the person who is lining you up with some business training, or that one business owner on Main Street who has been your mentor all along. Then get back to work!

If, however, you are a professional community practitioner, a volunteer community leader, a nonprofit administrator, an elected official or a service provider on the local or regional level, welcome! You've come to the right place. This is a book that discusses what *communities* can do to energize entrepreneurship in general and to support local entrepreneurs individually. You may be fortunate to already have others in your community who are looking at entrepreneurship as an economic development strategy. Many local leaders are enthusiastic about "gardening" rather than "hunting" to build their local economies. They are eager for the nuts and bolts of where to start and what to do. We believe the tools, the stories, the knowledge and the data compiled here will help.

Our Team

Two organizations have collaborated on E^2 *Energizing Entrepreneurs: Charting a Course for Rural Communities*. First is the Rural Policy Research Institute's Center for Rural Entrepreneurship, led by Don Macke, Deb Markley and Brian Dabson. Their field work throughout rural America has identified the need for a network of practitioners and a practical guide for community level work. Don and Deb authored many of the chapters dealing with economic history and entrepreneurship, as well as chapters on assessment, strategies and policy. The second organization is the Heartland Center for Leadership Development, which has a focus on community capacity building, evaluation and leadership development. Vicki Luther, Co-Director of the Heartland Center, contributed chapters on these topics, and Heartland Center Co-Director Milan Wall and other staff members served as copy editors.

The strengths of these two organizations are demonstrated in the wide range of examples from field work and the keen insights into what really needs to happen in a community in order to energize entrepreneurs. The stories and tools that illustrate concepts and strategies all come from the real life practice of these two organizations, and their network of other practitioners: people who live and work in communities that need to find ways to create wealth and new jobs; people who are well aware that recruiting a big employer from the outside is a long shot and a high risk; people who recognize that the *community* itself must play a leading role in making entrepreneurship *happen*.

Because so many community leaders and economic development practitioners have shared their experiences with us and supported our writing by providing great stories and tools, we feel that in many ways our audience has helped to construct this resource. And, we are indebted to all of you whose stories appear in these pages.

How to Use this Book

We would like you to think of this book as a resource that is like a road map for the landscape of rural entrepreneurship. A map has no beginning or end. It is designed for many different users, who begin at different places and are headed in different directions. While the chapters are organized sequentially, each can stand on its own to allow for various "entry points" you may choose, depending upon your own experience and where your community is, right now, regarding its support for entrepreneurs. You'll find that this book uses plain, non-academic language and is intended as a practical guide for building community entrepreneurship support systems. We expect that you will pick it up, put it down, open and close it often—studying and sharing these tools with others as you proceed along your course.

Finally, maps must be updated fairly often in order to reflect the changing world around us. The landscape of rural entrepreneurship is evolving at a rapid pace, with emerging success stories, creative local policies, and new technologies surfacing every day. Our intention is to revise this publication as often as is possible. In order to keep pace with our changing environment, an interactive website has been created as a special companion to this publication. People who are working in the field can learn from one another through our website at www.energizingentrepreneurs.org. There you will find many of the materials in this book, plus timely articles and reports from the field, and an invitation to contact us and become part of a growing network of practitioners across the nation who are energizing entrepreneurs.

An Overview of What's Ahead

To provide a basic context for the work of energizing entrepreneurs, we begin by describing the range of rural economic development in traditional practice and how this has changed throughout history. Chapter 2 focuses on historical trends and economic theories that have defined rural development. Working to create entrepreneurial communities in rural America requires an understanding of what rural is. We spend time in Chapter 3 discussing the important dimensions of working in rural places. Chapter 4 introduces us to several social and business entrepreneurs, and describes different types of entrepreneurs who make up a community's entrepreneurial talent pool.

Chapter 5 provides information that is vital to understanding why entrepreneurship has emerged as such an important strategy for rural communities. It also includes data that will help you make a case for embracing entrepreneurship as a core part of your community's economic development focus. Community leaders must be skilled at making this case in order to persuade others and to secure resources for this new focus.

Chapter 6 explores different stages of readiness in a community for energizing entrepreneurs. Readiness in this case means people and organizations, as well as political will. Chapter 7 describes several assessment instruments and how to actually use them to decide where to begin crafting your community's strategy for energizing entrepreneurs. In Chapter 8, we share with you what we've learned about successful entrepreneurship strategies and feature special sections on success stories from across the country.

In Chapter 9 we discuss community capacity, leadership development and youth engagement as cornerstones for maintaining momentum as we work for sustainable, entrepreneurial communities. The importance of "keeping score" is the focus of Chapter 10. It includes creative ways to measure your progress and report results to the community at large. With a long term economic development strategy like entrepreneurship, we need to find new ways to measure progress and we offer some examples of how you might do this in your community. This chapter also provides a detailed example of how you can address accountability for your funders and other community members.

Chapter 11 will help you connect your work to local policymakers so that the strategies you have developed can become part of your community's culture and institutions. It also describes several regions that have elevated rural entrepreneurship to the statewide policy arena. And we conclude *our* journey through rural entrepreneurship with suggestions on how you can begin *yours*. We'll wrap up the book in Chapter 12 by hitting the highpoints once again and sending you off with a pep talk for future action.

Each chapter also includes suggested resources (print as well as electronic) for further investigation. We hope that the reader's interest will be sparked by what is introduced in our publication and you will be encouraged to seek out more and deeper learning.

The Big Picture

Throughout our economic history we find entrepreneurial legends who have gone beyond their immediate personal goals to create stronger communities and a better society. Our expectations are, in fact, that entrepreneurs create more than just wealth for themselves and jobs for others. We encourage and support entrepreneurs because they have the creative potential to contribute to our quality of life. They are often people who have the vision and the energy to build better communities. They epitomize what we think of when we hear the phrase, "corporate citizenship." They are both business and civic entrepreneurs in our communities.

In the spring of 2005, 20 experienced entrepreneurship specialists—civic entrepreneurs—from across the United States gathered together for two days to analyze the framework we had established for this publication. They helped to describe in detail programs and strategies that represent a wide variety of model practices. We discussed challenges and success stores and tried to collect as many techniques and approaches as possible. Ultimately, we gained great insights that added richness to the development of this publication and our companion website. We are indebted to the Ewing Marion Kauffman Foundation for support of this special gathering.

Conversations during the practitioners' network informed our work on a much larger scale than just economic development. The gathering offered validation for our own insights. We view the process of entrepreneurship development as being about more than just encouraging private or business entrepreneurs. It's also about creating a community *environment* that is entrepreneurial—where entrepreneurship is embraced by public and civic organizations and their leaders.

Tom Lyons from the University of Louisville addressed an issue that was raised throughout many of our work sessions—the issue of how we tend to separate civic from business entrepreneurship. Maybe because we come from so many different backgrounds, some view entrepreneurs as targets, clients, or even customers. All of these suggest a *transaction:* We give you this service and you give us jobs. But is that really what we are after? Shouldn't we really be seeking a *transformation?* If we are to become "transforming agents" for our communities we will need to recast the way we look at our work in order to put together a unified way of thinking.

As collaborative partners for many years, and now as co-authors of this guide, the Heartland Center for Leadership Development and the RUPRI Center for Rural Entrepreneurship share a set of binding values that have brought our team together. Built on years of experience and understanding of rural culture and history, our team shares a set of cornerstone beliefs:

- People must have a say in the decisions that affect them.
- There is something special about both the strengths and challenges of rural communities.
- Rural communities must build upon their assets to achieve sustained economic development.
- Encouraging entrepreneurship, both private and civic, is vital to the future success of rural communities.
- Community level work must be tied to policy development.
- A learning community of practitioners is vital to continual

learning and improvement of community economic development.

As you chart your community course and begin to explore entrepreneurship as an intentional development approach, we hope you will join us in supporting these values as well. Both of our organizations invite you to visit our websites and learn about the types of training and capacity-building programs that we offer, in addition to our publications. Some are created and delivered in partnership and others with a single organizational focus. Please stop by any time!

**Heartland Center
for Leadership
Development**
www.heartlandcenter.info
800-927-1115

Center for RURAL
ENTREPRENEURSHIP
www.ruraleship.org
402-323-7339

CHAPTER 2
ECONOMIC
DEVELOPMENT TODAY

Just what rural America needs—another book on "how to do economic development." So many resources have been produced over the years and still so many rural communities are struggling and lacking economic opportunity.

We all know well that our world is changing rapidly. What made sense yesterday may not make sense today and clearly will be irrelevant tomorrow. Think about this reality for just one minute. The lifespan on the Fortune 500 (list of the United States largest corporations) is constantly shortening. Erik Pages with EntreWorks Consulting shares the numbers:

- In 1960 it took 35 years to replace 35% of the Fortune 500.
- In 1999 it took 3 to 4 years to do so!

If the largest corporations can't figure out how to stay on top, how can small rural communities even begin to compete?

Ensuring our communities' success into the future is challenging. The alternative is failure and decline. Understanding economic development today is critically important. For rural communities to compete, they must adopt a development strategy that is in tune with economic and social realities that are driving change in the early part of the 21st century.

Elements of Successful Development

Every farmer knows that you cannot reap what you do not sow. The same is true with economic development. Development will occur organically, but the nature, extent and equity of the development will likely vary widely. In today's rapidly changing world where uncertainty reigns, being intentional, yet flexible in economic development is critically important.

Successful development efforts are rooted in five core elements:

- **Vision**
- **Opportunity**
- **Asset-Based**
- **Investment**
- **Sustainability**

Let's explore each of these five core elements central to successful community economic development in the 21st century.

Vision

Our world is full of challenges and uncertainties. We cannot begin to control all the trends and issues that affect the success of our communities. However, field research is clear—communities that have strong and relevant visions for the future do better than ones that do not. Vision is about being intentional. It implies that a community takes the time and makes the effort to understand its context, its strengths and its weaknesses, and that it is willing to invest in its own perceived future. This same trait is a hallmark of entrepreneurs. The path to the future is not straight, but a clear and powerful vision moves a community into its future within an environment of challenges, unforeseen opportunities and undeserved crises.

Opportunity

Another hallmark of successful entrepreneurs is the ability to perceive and assess opportunities. We believe this is also the hallmark of successful communities. Such communities not only have eyes open for new opportunities, but they also are actively scouting for them. Just as with entrepreneurs, successful communities do not pursue all opportunities. They acquire the collective skill for assessing perceived opportunities and pursuing those that make sense. Most successful communities rely on civic leaders to do this organically. However, in the 21st century, communities must step up one level and create an organized capacity to identify and assess opportunity.

Asset-Based

Every community has its challenges and its assets. Larger communities that are well positioned in the world seem to have all the advantages. Smaller, more isolated and rural communities might be perceived as having no assets. John McKnight at Northwestern University helped reinvent community development thinking with his research about asset-based development. He demonstrated that even the most distressed, poverty stricken and crime riddled urban neighborhoods have development assets. Successful communities in the 21st century are those that can map their assets and build a development strategy through an asset-based approach. Simply put, these communities build on what they have today, creating additional capacity to do more tomorrow.

Investment

To understand community investment, let's compare communities to successful corporations that annually reinvest in their own companies. Imagine a community of 5,000 people with a $750 million annual economy whose residents are willing to reinvest just five percent each year ($37.5 million annually) to renovate their homes, improve their streets and parks, build better schools, and invest in their local businesses.

Successful communities have always been willing to invest. Communities where public and private investments renew institutions also provide the best infrastructure and ever-competitive businesses. These are communities that learn to invest smartly in those things that will ensure future development and competitive advantage. Implied here are communities that strategically plan and are externally connected. Such communities are in a stronger position to know where to invest and how to make the case that supports necessary investment.

Sustainability

There are several constants, including the fact that our world and our position in the world are continually changing. Successful communities are entrepreneurial in reinventing themselves to ensure economic relevance. Successful communities are able to sustain development efforts in both good and bad times, thereby renewing themselves.

Sustainability has many facets, including leadership, civic capacity, health of public institutions, adequacy of infrastructure and private investment in business competitiveness. Many rural communities come up short because they cannot sustain development efforts. In times of crisis, they gear up and invest heavily, but they slack off when times improve. President Dwight D. Eisenhower, in his 1958 State of the Union address, said it best:

"Our real problem, then, is not our strength today;
it is rather the vital necessity of action today
to ensure our strength tomorrow."

Taken together, vision, opportunity, assets, investment and sustainability are the keys to successful long-term development in rural communities today as in the past.

Of course, there is actually another factor—luck. A bit of good luck can go a long way toward moving a development agenda forward. The key is the ability to perceive good luck when it strikes.

Other resources explore the history of development in far greater depth than we will in this book. However, we think it is important to share some history in order to provide a context for successful development today.

Historical Perspective

The history of rural economic development is one of change. It is a history of how people react and adapt to the different ways wealth is created in rural places. A clear pattern of development waves has shaped rural America through four distinct economic periods:

- **Subsistence Economies**
- **Natural Resources**
- **Business Attraction**
- **Urban Outsourcing**

Subsistence Economies

The first Americans were well suited to subsistence economies tied to the natural resources of their regions.

Hundreds of Native American tribes populated the North American continent, and their economies were rooted in hunting, gathering and small-scale farming. The majority of these communities gave way as European American settlements closed the frontier. Many tribes were relocated and some even brought to the point of extinction through genocide and cultural assimilation.

Natural Resources

Historically, European American development and wealth creation in rural America was directly and powerfully connected to natural resources. To illustrate this economic period, consider one agricultural state, Nebraska, from 1860 to 1890. In 1860, Nebraska's landscape was controlled and dominated by subsistence-based Native American communities. Roughly 29,000 European American settlers hugged the southeastern shores of the Missouri River. By 1890, the European American population of Nebraska had skyrocketed to over one million, 37 times its 1860 population. During these three decades, more than 800 new communities were established and over one-half million new farms and businesses created.

The driving force was natural resources. In Nebraska's case it was farm and ranch land. In other parts of rural America, the natural resources driving development were energy, minerals, timber, fisheries and eventually tourism. Natural resources formed the foundation of the economies and societies of most of rural America into the later decades of the 20th century.

As we move into the early decades of the 21st century, the economic rationale of rural communities created by natural resource utilization is eroding rapidly (with the clear exception of tourism).

Even as the last farms and ranches were being established in Nebraska, community leaders understood that economic diversification through industrial development was critically important. The same was true in other landscapes as communities sought to develop local industries (often tied to adding value to local natural resources) or through the attraction of branch plants and industries.

Business Attraction

World War II was one of those events that fundamentally changed America—particularly rural America. Rural Americans by the millions left their isolated and secure rural communities and discovered the larger world. These rural Americans gained new insights, perspectives and connections. World War II also greatly increased the industrial capacity of the United States. Following World II three trends greatly changed America and particularly rural America. First, the baby boom drove U.S. demographic growth. Second, pent-up consumer demand during World War II drove consumer spending following the war. Third, American corporations sought cheaper labor and land and began relocating America's factories to rural locations. Branch plant relocation brought economic diversification and growth to thousands of rural communities between the mid-1940s and contemporary times.

While industry continues to be important to rural America, the expansion of industrial output and the location of branch plants into rural America is a declining trend today. Industries that once would have located in rural America now are being built in Mexico, India and China. Business attraction opportunities still exist, but the development opportunity is a shadow of itself as compared to 20 or even 10 years ago.

As with all development waves, a new wave overlays the old wave. Natural resources and branch plants continue to be important, but they are largely unable to drive new wealth creation in the 21st century for most rural communities.

Urban Outsourcing

The most recent development wave might be referred to as "urban outsourcing." Its central theme is the location of economic activities in rural areas that urban areas do not want in their backyards. Here are some examples of urban outsourcing:
- Waste Management and Processing Facilities
- Energy Farms (e.g., wind farms)
- Prisons
- Food Processing (e.g., livestock slaughter)
- Back Office Shops (e.g., telemarketing)

Urban outsourcing can create economic opportunities, but such development also creates challenges for rural areas. Such facilities can often overwhelm the social fabric of smaller rural places, create huge tax obligations without expanded tax bases and provide short-term economic benefits. Urban outsourcing is unlikely to create the kind of long-term wealth creation and development that natural resource based industries and branch plant relocation offered rural America.

So, what does this mean for communities and their development? For one, development is a lot easier if you are moving with the current instead of against it. Natural resource industries like farming, ranching, mining, energy production, fishing and forestry continue to be important, but they offer limited ability to increase economic relevance, let alone prosperity, in an age where knowledge is valued. Industrial development is fundamental, and key industries like manufacturing are likely to be with us for many years to come. However, industrial development is a maturing sector with limited growth potential.

The application of knowledge to these traditional and emerging industries is where opportunities for development, new wealth creation and economic justification are rooted for communities today and into the future.

The question remains, what kind of development offers inherent and long-term opportunities for rural America in the 21st century? Let's explore the possibilities.

Where Our Future Rests

Kevin Phillips traces the creation of wealth over modern history in his book, *Wealth and Democracy*. A summary of this and other works suggests that new wealth is rooted in two sources— old wealth and innovation/creativity.

In market economies wealth tends to concentrate. We generally call this old wealth. Old wealth has the advantage of creating new wealth through passive investments in stocks, bonds, real estate and other opportunities. The vast majority of rural Americans who do not have the advantage of old wealth rely on hard work and smarts to create new wealth. The same is true with communities.

Every community has old wealth tied to the assets of current and former residents. Community foundations throughout rural

America are helping their communities connect to donors who hold this old wealth by creating legacy endowments to support new wealth creation. Effectively mobilizing old wealth is a critical source of new investment for rural communities today. With diminishing government support systems, this may represent the most important future investment source available to rural communities.

However, for most communities, the key to success in the 21st century is to support innovation that offers the opportunity for new wealth creation. Entrepreneurs have been with us for a very long time. Entrepreneurs create new wealth for themselves and their communities by taking innovations to market and commercializing new ideas to meet consumer desires. In a very interesting study, *From the Garage to the Boardroom: The Entrepreneurial Roots of America's Largest Corporations*, the National Commission on Entrepreneurship explored the origins of the Fortune 200 in the United States between 1917 and 1987. What they found is fascinating and informing. Entrepreneurs created over one-half of all the Fortune 200 corporations during this period. This finding illustrates the power of entrepreneurs to discover innovation and create successful ventures around it.

Helping local entrepreneurs succeed represents one of the more promising development strategies in the 21st century. You might ask—how do we get our heads around this new development opportunity? Our community understands farming, timber and business attraction. Where do we go to understand how helping local entrepreneurs can create development, economic opportunity and wealth for our community? Let's explore some examples and stories.

Places to Watch

Jack Schultz, a developer from Effingham, Illinois, gives us a great place to begin our journey toward understanding the entrepreneurial opportunity for development. In his book, *Boom Town USA*, Jack identifies some of the most successful rural communities today. The vast majority of these communities share one key characteristic—they are entrepreneurial. Most have now discovered the importance of supporting local entrepreneurs.

The RUPRI Center for Rural Entrepreneurship has identified a number of communities throughout the country that are actively embracing entrepreneurship-based economic development strategies. Throughout this book, we'll share stories of places as diverse as Littleton, Colorado, and Douglas, Georgia; Humboldt County, California, and North Central Kansas; Jefferson County, Washington, and Valley County, Nebraska; Fairfield, Iowa, and Appalachian Ohio.

We also encourage you to explore your own region and discover communities that are entrepreneurial and embracing entrepreneurship as a core development strategy.

Additional Resources

You can't build a strategy without access to resources. At the end of each chapter, you'll find this section, Additional Resources, to help you continue your efforts to energize entrepreneurs in your communities.

Your first stop for more information is the *E² Energizing Entrepreneurs* website, www.energizingentrepreneurs.org. Once there, click on "Economic Development Today" to find resources that support the information in this chapter.

We also recommend the following resources:

Boom Town USA: The 71/2 Keys to Big Success in Small Towns is a must read for all small town leaders. Written by Jack Schultz, an economic developer with plenty of experience in small town America, this book provides not only great insight—it is inspirational as well. National Association of Industrial and Office Properties. 2004. www.naiop.org

Building Entrepreneurial Communities: The Appropriate Role of Enterprise Development Activities puts enterprise development into the broader context of community building. Written by Gregg Lichtenstein, Tom Lyons, and Nailya Kutzhanova, this paper reflects the many years of experience that the authors have working in the field of enterprise development.

CHAPTER 3
WORKING IN
RURAL AMERICA

A Story from Big City Atlanta

In 2004, the National Business Incubation Association (NBIA) annual conference was held in Atlanta, Georgia. By almost anyone's definition, Atlanta is a big city and as far away from rural America as you can get. Just before the conference, a leading venture capital investment firm requested some help in exploring investing in rural America. These experts wanted to learn more about rural areas. As part of the conversation, the venture capital staff was asked to define rural America in their own terms and they responded...

> *"When we think of rural America,*
> *we think of places maybe like Lincoln, Nebraska,*
> *and definitely Omaha, Nebraska."*

For reference purposes, Lincoln, Nebraska, is now a city of 250,000 and the Omaha metro area now exceeds 650,000!

When we think of rural, we visualize places like Dickinson, North Dakota (16,000), Mullen, Nebraska (450), Fairfield, Iowa (9,500), or Douglas, Georgia (10,600). Obviously, there is a real disconnect between perceptions of rural and realities. Working in Mullen or Douglas is a whole lot different than working in Lincoln or Omaha.

What is Rural?

Every community is unique and offers a special set of challenges. Understanding the nature and character of a landscape is fundamental to developing it effectively. We begin our exploration of *Working in Rural America* with a search for a definition of rural.

Rural America accounts for between 70% and 80% of the geographic area of the United States. Roughly 55 million Americans (about 20%) call rural home. Rural America's economic and cultural contributions fall somewhere between these two statistics—greater than the population base would suggest, but less than the geographic ratio.

Finally, there is a sociological rural America with major implications for development. We all have our ideas, images, and biases when we hear the word "rural" or think about rural places. However, as America has become more demographically and culturally urban, our clarity of understanding of "what is rural" has diminished.

This question seems more important to non-rural organizations working in rural, than to folks from rural places. The question is most likely rooted in the desire to better define whether policies and programs need to be customized or changed to meet "rural" circumstances. We'll provide a framework, rather than a strict definition, to more effectively inform our work in rural places.

In a simple way, everyone knows rural America when they see it and experience it. Rural America is really a patchwork quilt of places and communities that are richly diverse. This diversity challenges us as we attempt to explore how development can enrich rural America. There is no one clear and compelling definition of rural America. There are, in fact, numerous and often conflicting definitions. We will attempt to create a framework for rural America by exploring it in four different ways:

- **Demographically**
- **Spatially**
- **Sociologically**
- **Economically**

Demographic Rural America

The U.S. federal government has a number of definitions based on demographic considerations. In recent years, agencies such as the U.S. Census Bureau, the U.S. Department of Agriculture and the U.S. Department of Housing and Urban Development have employed the following definitions based on size of place:

- Rural—Open country and places with 2,500 or fewer residents
- Urban—Places with more than 2,500 but fewer than 50,000 residents
- Metropolitan—Places with greater than 50,000 residents

Non-metropolitan—often a reference point for rural—is the inverse of metropolitan—places with fewer than 50,000 residents. However, there is a world of difference between a community of 250 in eastern Montana and a trade center in Iowa with 35,000 residents.

The U.S. Office of Management and Budget is changing our definitions of place with the addition of *micropolitan* places. Micropolitan places are basically the larger trade center communities located in rural America. This new statistical category will, in effect, reduce the number of people and communities that are "counted" as rural.

Spatial Rural America

For a number of years, America has been divided into 10 spatial types. The "Beale Code" (named after the system's founder, Norman Beale of the Economic Research Service in the U.S. Department of Agriculture) is based on a continuum from central city to isolated rural. The Beale Code classifications are as follows:

0 Central Counties – Metro – 1 million or more residents
1 Fringe Counties – Metro – 1 million or more residents
2 Metro – 250,000 to 1 million residents
3 Metro – Less than 250,000 residents
4 Urban – 20,000 or more residents – Metro Adjacent
5 Urban – 20,000 or more residents – Not Metro Adjacent
6 Urban – 2,500 to 20,000 residents – Metro Adjacent
7 Urban – 2,500 to 20,000 residents – Not Metro Adjacent
8 Rural – Less than 2,500 residents – Metro Adjacent
9 Rural – Less than 2,500 residents – Not Metro Adjacent

REDEFINING RURAL AMERICA

Rural places that have prospered and grown have become, by definition, either urban, micropolitan, or perhaps even metropolitan.

The process of economic development can lead to a decline in the number of places that we call "rural." The most prosperous rural communities "grow out" of what we define as rural. Often, it is the most challenged regions that remain, resulting in a rural America that is defined by population decline, poverty and lack of economic vitality.

By almost anyone's standard, category nine is rural. There are two major problems with the Beale Code. First, it is based on counties. In many parts of America, but particularly in the West where counties are huge geographically, a county may be defined as metro, yet still have vast rural areas. Second, with the proposed federal Office of Management and Budget changes, the relevance of the Beale Code may be undermined.

Sociological Rural America

In today's world, with universal communications, fashion, and media, regional customs and values are eroding. One must be particularly isolated to remain disconnected from the universal world culture of the 21st century. Despite cultural globalization, there remain unique sociological differences. John Allen, director of the Western Rural Development Center, in Logan, Utah, has summarized extensive research into a set of urban and rural cultural values. These are summarized as follows:

Value Attribute	Rural	Urban
Community Interaction	Mandatory	Voluntary
Roles	Ascribed	Achieved
Sanctions	Particularistic	Universalistic
Orientation	Group	Individual
Leadership	Traditional	Rational

The reality is that a community may be rural demographically (because it is small) or spatially (because it is isolated) or economically (because of its industry mix), but have an urban sociology. For those rural places that continue to have rural value attributes, the implications for development are significant. These values contribute to the conservative nature of many rural places.

Rural America's Economy

Rural America's economy is as diverse as it is physically large. Traditionally, this economic activity has fallen into one of the following sectors: natural resource industries, processing and manufacturing industries, corridor industries, government-related activities, and local support activities. Generally, most of rural

America's core economic activities are rooted more in old economies than new economies.

NATURAL RESOURCE INDUSTRIES. Predominant among rural America's economic sectors are the natural resource industries of farming, ranching, timbering, mining, energy production, and fisheries. When active and well resourced, these industries can create wealth and active economies. However, as resources are depleted, recession and decline undermine vitality.

PROCESSING INDUSTRIES. Closely associated with the natural resources and open spaces found in rural America are processing and manufacturing industries that need raw materials, unskilled and semi-skilled workforces, and space to operate. While these industries remain important to rural America, many are in decline because of depleted resources and the transition of manufacturing jobs to countries with lower wage scales and fewer environmental regulations.

CORRIDOR INDUSTRIES. Most Americans now live in either suburbs (roughly one in two Americans live in the suburbs) or central cities (where about one in four Americans live). These places require connection to each other and the rest of the world. Because rural America exists between metropolitan areas, a central economic activity is serving as a transportation and communication corridor. Railroads, highways, pipelines, and fiber optics all cross rural America and are creating secondary economic activity.

GOVERNMENT-RELATED INDUSTRIES. The federal government (and to a lesser extent state government) is a major economic player in rural America. The public sector owns and operates vast tracks of public lands, such as national forests, military installations, prisons, and waste sites. In addition to government land ownership and activities, the NGO sector (non-governmental organizations) has an increasing presence in rural America. For example, the Nature Conservancy now works in more than 500 rural landscapes throughout America.

SUPPORT ACTIVITIES. Finally, there are assorted economic activities that support communities and their needs. Local government, retail, personal services, health care, and education all fall into this category. Emerging research suggests that, although deteriorating rural communities suffer from a lack of incoming wealth, it is their inability to *capture and recycle* the incoming wealth that has the greater negative effect.

Rural communities that are more isolated and struggling are, in many ways, reflections of the past. This rural America is defined by an historic economy, which in turn shaped its communities, societies and cultures. Creating a new future will require these communities to break free from their past. At the end of this chapter, we share some thoughts on sectors that may have the potential to create economic development in rural areas. As you read this section, we encourage you to open your mind and think outside the box about the economic opportunities that may exist in your community!

New and Potential Economic Drivers in Rural America

We have identified six economic drivers that are affecting vast areas within rural America and have the potential to impact rural economies in both positive and negative ways. The direction of this impact may well hinge on the ability of community leaders to recognize and plan for the changes these trends will bring.

SUBURBANIZATION. In terms of dollar value, activity level and impact, the single largest economic force in rural America today is suburbanization. We love what cities offer, but more and more Americans are pushing further out into the adjoining rural countryside to live and raise their families. In time, the city catches up and incorporates these developing areas, transforming them from a rural to an urban landscape. This transformation brings competitive challenges as well as economic opportunities to rural communities.

SEASONAL RESIDENTS. A recent story in the *Denver Post* reported that 1.3 million people live in rural forested areas of

Colorado. Since the turn of the 19th century, Americans have increasingly selected metropolitan areas for their primary homes. However, over the past quarter century these same Americans have chosen rural landscapes for their recreational, retirement and second homes. Rural acreages, subdivisions and entire new communities are growing rapidly not only in high amenity areas, but even in more remote areas such as the Great Plains. Again, the growth in this sector brings both challenges and opportunities to rural places.

ELDER INDUSTRIES. The single fastest growing demographic group in rural America (for that matter in all of America) is elders, defined here as persons 65 years of age and older. Most elders are relatively affluent or middle class. They have resources, spending power and considerable political power. The aging baby boom demographic (the single largest group in American history) is driving the creation of entire new industries to meet their needs.

LONE EAGLES. The Center for the New West coined the term *Lone Eagles*. The trend line is clear and strong—many, many urban Americans are moving to rural settings and making their livings via the Internet. We do not fully understand the economic and social impacts that Lone Eagles will have on rural communities, but growing evidence suggests that this is a trend worth monitoring. Lone Eagles may become the next generation of business and community leaders, community philanthropists, and mentors for emerging entrepreneurs and youth in our rural communities.

ENTREPRENEURIAL GROWTH COMPANIES (EGCs). The U.S. Department of Labor delineates 394 economic regions in the United States. According to research by the National Commission on Entrepreneurship, every one of these regions has EGCs. These EGCs, or "gazelles," are the companies that are achieving rapid and sustained growth and are the engines of regional economic performance. Supporting existing EGCs and helping other growth-oriented entrepreneurial companies to achieve EGC status may represent a core rural development opportunity.

TECHNOLOGICAL ADVANCEMENT. Rural economies continue to be influenced by the rapid advancement of technology, particularly telecommunications. Lone Eagles work from remote locations via broadband access to the Internet. Main Street businesses tap national markets by using advanced telecommunications. These advancements make it easier for rural entrepreneurs to reach regional, national and even international markets while raising the competitive stakes for rural businesses.

Implications for Our Work

Okay—there is no single definition of rural. Rural America is a very diverse set of places with complex histories, economies and cultural orientations. So, what does this really matter to communities that want to build stronger economies through entrepreneurship? It makes all the difference in the world! Development should be culturally appropriate. We know that is true from our failed efforts in the developing world. However, this lesson is true for inner city neighborhoods and rural areas, as well. By understanding the place we are trying to develop, we have a greater chance of succeeding.

Understanding a place's history, its current economy and even its demographic trends is relatively easy. All these considerations are important and form the context in which development is undertaken. All have implications for creating an environment for entrepreneurs. However, understanding the sociology of a community is paramount.

The conservative and risk–adverse nature of rural places harbors great implications for creating more entrepreneurial economies in rural America. When rural people are profiled according to entrepreneurial attributes, the result is mixed. In general, rural people have strong entrepreneurial attributes related to independence, resourcefulness and initiative. However, these same characteristics may inhibit their willingness to network and partner. Working from John Allen's research, we offer the following insights:

Anonymity

A central element that contributes to differentiated urban/rural values is the degree of anonymity that individuals enjoy within the community where they work and live. Persons located in larger urban communities enjoy a greater level of anonymity compared with persons residing in smaller communities, where it is difficult to remain anonymous. For entrepreneurs, the lack of anonymity makes it harder to fail (or to be wildly successful) without undergoing intense community scrutiny.

Community Interaction

In urban places, community interaction is voluntary with lower expectations for engagement. In rural communities, one is expected to be involved in the life of the community. This can range from the simple obligation to wave or say hello, to the requirements of full community engagement. To not be involved can bring on sanctions and marginal status. For a rural entrepreneur who is fully engaged in creating and growing an enterprise, this focused behavior can be perceived as disconnecting from the community, thus violating community norms.

Roles

In urban communities, roles are achieved through good work, and good connections. In rural communities, roles are often ascribed. If the parents are farmers, it may be hard for the community to accept the next generation in another role. Ascribed roles may limit the ability of a rural person to try something new and undermine the community's ability to support new roles. Given that entrepreneurs are interested in the process and outcomes of creation—not necessarily being a banker, teacher, or some other ascribed role—it may be hard for an entrepreneur to thrive in such an environment.

Sanctions

The value of sanctions actually works in favor of entrepreneurial development. In rural communities, sanctions are particularistic, based on the individual and their particular history in the community. For example, a person may be an inven-

UNDERSTANDING THE ENVIRONMENT

Understanding the mix of rural/urban values within a particular region or community can greatly help in building a more entrepreneurial climate. Furthermore, working within these values can enable a more sustainable development effort

tor and business creator with a mixed history of failure and success. If the community has accepted this behavior, it may be very supportive as long as accounts are balanced during successful periods, offsetting the anti-social behavior associated with failures.

Orientation

In urban places, the orientation is individualistic. In rural places, the orientation is toward the "group," such as a church, the downtown merchants, or a community service club. The implications of this value for entrepreneurs are two-fold. If the group is supportive, a very positive climate can be created for the entrepreneur. If, however, the orientation is also parochial, it may prevent the entrepreneur from reaching outside of his or her group to network, to find markets or create strategic alliances.

Leadership

Finally, the leadership model in rural places tends to be traditional versus the rational model in urban places. For example, in rural places there is the formal leadership ascribed with roles—the mayor, school superintendent, banker, or rich person on the hill. This is traditional leadership. Within these communities, there are also builders—folks who can get things done. They tend to work below the surface and behave in ways that are accepted by traditional leadership. If traditional leadership is supportive, a positive entrepreneurial climate can be created within the community. For rural communities that are conservative, the role of traditional leaders is often to ensure that the community does not mess up (the price of failure is higher in smaller rural places). This conservator role can, in turn, inhibit entrepreneurial behavior.

The bottom line is that rural places may have less growth, fewer high growth entrepreneurs and a community culture that is less than supportive of entrepreneurial creativity. Those of us who live and work in rural communities must find the time to take stock of our community. By understanding our current environment better, we stand a stronger chance of building a more supportive environment for our entrepreneurs.

Shifting the Economic Development Paradigm in Rural America

Entrepreneurs are good at thinking outside the box, or more appropriately, looking at reality differently, which allows them to see market opportunities most of us miss. They embrace, manage and respond to change in a way that continually moves their ventures forward. We have historically organized our economy in certain ways, and our means of measuring success are based on that old framework. However, change has no respect for old ways of doing the business of economic development.

Community leaders in rural America must become more entrepreneurial in the way they think about economic development. Leadership from both private and civic entrepreneurs will be needed to embrace a new economic development paradigm in rural America. Private entrepreneurs are very good at seeing the opportunities that lie in the emerging sectors described above. Given the right support, these entrepreneurs will create the new ventures that can transform the rural economy. It is the job of enlightened community leaders to become civic entrepreneurs— to recognize what is driving your local community, to think innovatively and creatively about promising new sectors, and to implement strategies that encourage and support the development of private entrepreneurs.

Rural America has been, and will continue to be, challenged by economic trends and changes. However, armed with information about the rural economy, community leaders can embrace a new way of thinking about economic development and begin to develop and implement strategies to create supportive entrepreneurial environments in their rural hometowns.

Thinking Outside the Box about the Rural Economy

As we described earlier in this chapter, rural economies continue to be dominated by sectors that are more strongly connected to the old economy than to the new economy. However, there are some sectors—existing, emerging, and potential—that may provide new economic development opportunities for rural communities. While some of these sectors may be familiar to you and your community, others require you to think more creatively about the opportunities they may hold for your local economy.

RECREATIONAL TOURISM. One traditional economic sector with high growth potential is recreational tourism. This is a diverse and complicated sector with literally thousands of emerging niche markets. Although recreational tourism tends to concentrate in traditional high-amenity rural areas (e.g., mountains, lakes, coastal areas), it is also reaching more diverse areas, such as Delta Arkansas or rural grasslands. New ideas about eco-tourism are bringing birders and other nature-minded visitors to all parts of rural America.

HYDROCARBON FEEDSTOCK. A growing percentage of agricultural and nonagricultural commodities are being produced today as hydrocarbon feedstock. Corn, soybeans and timber are all harvested and extensively processed to produce ingredients for everything from soy ink to paper to sweeteners. Crops with specific genetic engineering are being produced to meet specific food, fiber, chemical and pharmaceutical needs.

BACK OFFICE CENTERS. Although creative, productive and corporate centers remain in America's largest cities, more of the back office operations are moving off shore and in some cases to rural America. Back office operations range from call centers to accounting services to paperwork processing and storage. Many firms are finding a willing workforce and welcoming communities for this type of economic development.

ARTISANS. One aspect of globalization is standardization. While national shopping malls only want well-known franchises, there is a counter movement centered on uniqueness and artistic drive. Throughout rural America, individuals are engaged in making arts and crafts. Often small in scale, artisan activities are reaching industry proportions through marketing associations, retail outlets and cooperatives.

NEW GENERATION NATURAL RESOURCE INDUSTRIES. Within the highly concentrated commodity-based industries that farming, ranching, forestry and fisheries have become, there is a new generation of ventures focused on product, not commodity. These small ventures are producing organic wheat, grass-fed beef, free-range poultry, furniture from restoration timber and seafood for urban eateries. While the potential for these often marginal ventures is unclear, it is worth watching.

ALTERNATIVE ENERGY PRODUCTION.   Power shortages and high oil prices remind us of the energy crisis days of the 1970s. Wind power farms and other forms of solar energy production are making a comeback in some rural landscapes. Again, we are not sure of the long-term prospect of harvesting rural America's solar and wind resources for energy production, but enough is taking place to stay tuned.

CARBON SEQUESTRATION.   Although the international debate over global warming will continue, the removal of carbon from the atmosphere through growing vegetation like forests and grasses is fundamental to countering global warming. Scenarios suggest that there may be more economic value in restoring tall grass prairies for carbon sequestration than for growing corn. This market is new and may never mature, but it could change the economic choices for how we use rural landscapes.

Additional Resources

For more information visit the E^2 *Energizing Entrepreneurs* website, www.energizingentrepreneurs.org. Once there, click on "Working in Rural America" to find resources that support the information in this chapter.

All that has been written about rural America could fill a large library.   Few of us have the time to become true scholars of rural America.   However, if you would like to deepen your understanding just a bit more we suggest the following five resources:

Your Field Guide to Community Building by Vicki Luther and Mary Emery, Heartland Center for Leadership Development. This is a practical resource for any community leader.   It covers the basics of working at the community level. Copies of the guide can be purchased at www.heartlandcenter.info.

Community Economics: Linking Theory and Practice by Ron Shaffer, Steve Deller and Dave Marcouiller. These guys have it right and this book provides just what it says—a link between theory and practice. Blackwell Publishing.

Rural Communities: Legacy and Change by Cornelia Butler Flora and Jan L. Flora with Susan Fey. Jan and Neal Flora have defined community civic capacity and provided great insight into what makes communities successful. This book captures decades of learning and insights. Westview Press.

The Failure of National Rural Policy by William P. Browne. Ill-conceived and poorly executed national policy has played the central role in the decline of rural America. This book does a sound job of capturing this element of important history. Georgetown University Press.

Rural Development in the United States: Connecting Theory, Practice, and Possibilities, by William A. Galston and Haren J. Baehler, is a classic. Island Press.

CHAPTER 4
ENTREPRENEURS AND
ENTREPRENEURSHIP

An Entrepreneur is Born in Rural Washington

Mike Reichner is somewhat of an impulsive guy. After he and his wife, Jadyne, bought property on Washington's Olympic Peninsula, Mike attended a community meeting on growing lavender. "He came home and announced that we were going to start a lavender farm," Jadyne said. Being the analytical half of the team, she researched lavender and found that it was a promising possibility. In 1996, they sold their boat and borrowed $4,000 from Jadyne's mother for an irrigation system and 19 lavender plants. They traded and borrowed equipment, and friends helped ditch in pipes. And so in the Dungeness Valley on Bell Bottom Road, Purple Haze Lavender was born.

Over the past five years, our team has traveled over one million miles throughout rural America. We have crossed paths with many remarkable people like Mike and Jadyne. The power of entrepreneurs to see and create successful ventures around them is simply amazing. In so many ways, Mike and Jadyne embody the true characteristics of rural entrepreneurs and fly in the face of popular myths. Mike was a state park superintendent and Jadyne was a science teacher. They were wage and salary folks seeking retirement in a beautiful valley in Washington State's rain shadow near Sequim. However, like all successful entrepreneurs, they had passion and a dream. Retirement could wait a bit longer. They acquired the knowledge and skills to succeed in the business world. The motivation to create businesses like Purple Haze Lavender must be rooted deeply in the personalities of entrepreneurs. Business skills can be learned if the passion runs deep enough. Incidentally, those first 19 lavender plants grew into a multi-million dollar business.

Entrepreneurs and this creative process we call entrepreneurship play a central role in all our lives. Entrepreneurs create not only better lives for themselves and their families, but they also represent a driving force in our society and economy. They envision and create businesses that meet our material needs in interesting and more effective ways. Other entrepreneurs create remarkable communities through great schools, parks, libraries and other public services that enrich our quality of life.

Entrepreneurs – Who Are They?

When the word entrepreneur is spoken, everyone in the room has an image of what that word means. To some, entrepreneurs are only the high growth wizards like Bill Gates with Microsoft or Sam Walton with Wal-Mart. To others, the word equates to "small business" or "microenterprise." For some the image is a struggling startup that never equates to meaningful economic development.

If we are to develop our communities through entrepreneurship, then we must dig a bit deeper and better understand who entrepreneurs are and how we can help them succeed, thereby enriching our communities. We offer three lenses for gaining a deeper understanding of who entrepreneurs are, beginning with some common definitions, continuing with some portraits of rural entrepreneurs, and wrapping up with a workable typology to guide our work.

Lens #1 A Few Definitions

ENTREPRENEURSHIP AND ENTREPRENEURS DEFINED

"Entrepreneurship is the transformation of an idea into an opportunity."

–Jeff Timmons, Babson College

"Any attempt to create a new business enterprise or to expand an established business."

–Jay Kayne, Miami University

"Essential agents of change who accelerate the generation, application and spread of innovative ideas and in doing so…not only ensure efficient use of resources, but also expand the boundaries of economic activity.

–Global Entrepreneurship Monitor

Listed here are some of the commonly used definitions of entrepreneurs and entrepreneurship. The bottom line is that all the definitions share the same central characteristics: a focus on opportunities and the creation of ventures. Like reality, there is rich diversity of entrepreneurs, from the bright-eyed startup to the seasoned veteran launching an expansion.

Here is our favorite definition of an entrepreneur:

"Entrepreneurs perceive new opportunities and create and grow ventures around such opportunities."

Several points about the meaning of entrepreneurs and entrepreneurship warrant emphasis. First, entrepreneurship is all about specific individuals or groups of individuals, not businesses. The outcome of entrepreneurship is a successful commercial or philanthropic venture, but our focus is on the person who engages in this creative process—the entrepreneur. Second, small business owners are not necessarily entrepreneurs. According to the National Commission on Entrepreneurship (NCOE), only 4%–5% of American firms account for high growth companies and most are small businesses, according to the U.S. Small

Business Administration's definition. The difference between most small businesses and entrepreneurial small businesses is the orientation and capacity of the owner/operator with respect to innovation and growth.

Lens #2 Five Entrepreneurs

Entrepreneurs are specific people who engage in the creative process. We can talk about entrepreneurs in abstract terms, but that will never have an impact on our communities. Eventually, we need to identify and learn about the entrepreneurs in our community. To help this process of discovery, we'd like to introduce you to five entrepreneurs from rural America:

- **Maxine Moul of Nebraska**
- **Larry Comer of Georgia**
- **Pam Curry of West Virginia**
- **Beth Strube of North Dakota**
- **The Kentucky Highlands Investment Corporation**

**Maxine Moul
Civic Entrepreneur
Lincoln, Nebraska**

Maxine and her husband Francis are journalists. They had a dream of owning their own newspaper. The chance presented itself and they used the three Fs (family, friends and fools) to raise the funds necessary to purchase the weekly newspaper in Syracuse, Nebraska (population 1,762). They not only succeeded with this venture, but they also created the Penny Press, a multi-state want-ad publication. By all standards Maverick Media and Francis and Maxine Moul were highly successful entrepreneurs and business people. Those family, friends, and fools who took a risk with the Mouls did really well when Maverick Media was sold. But our story about Maxine is not focused on her business successes—it is about her role as a *civic* entrepreneur. Maxine went on to become Nebraska's Lieutenant Governor and the Director of Nebraska's state economic development agency. However, her true civic legacy is in the creation of the Nebraska Community Foundation. NCF, as it is called, has become one of America's most successful and innovative rural community foundations. Maxine played the central role in its early creation and growth.

As a child growing up in Americus, Georgia, Larry Comer liked to play Monopoly. In this small farming community, he dreamed of running his own business. He admired his uncle, who worked long hours in a pipe fitting firm and then started a sprinkler company in the 1930s. In 1964, back in Americus, Comer started Metalux, a commercial and industrial lighting manufacturer. By 1985 when Larry sold Metalux, it had grown to $60 million in sales nationwide with more than 1,100 employees. Two years later Larry bought a struggling company called Caravelle Power Boats. He revived the ailing company and sold it in 1998. Like many entrepreneurs, Larry invested in other ventures. He was civic-minded, serving on the Georgia State Chamber of Commerce and other groups. However, Larry's greatest legacy may be his willingness to share. Throughout his life, he has mentored others seeking to own their own businesses. Larry Comer is a remarkable human being. He is creative and he is a premier entrepreneur. Most importantly, his impact on his community is multi-dimensional.

**Larry Comer
Business
Entrepreneur
Americus, Georgia**

Our next entrepreneur is Pam Curry of West Virginia. Like Larry, she is quiet, determined, and she is changing her corner of the world for the better.

Pam Curry's West Virginia home, as romanticized by John Denver's lyrics, inspires her life's work as a social entrepreneur. "West Virginia is my home and I have no plans to leave," Curry said from her office at the Center for Economic Options (CEO) in Charleston, West Virginia. The Center for Economic Options not only creates economic opportunities for entrepreneurial artisans in West Virginia; it also enriches the cultural life of this rural state.

Curry, CEO's executive director, spent decades watching family and friends who were forced to move because of the lack of economic opportunity: the diminishing coal industry, the absence of corporate headquarters and the distance to a large metropolitan area. "So many of us have left the state, always hoping to come back," Curry said, pointing out that her father-in-law, a coal-miner, relocated his family to Cleveland to work in the auto industry before finally moving back. Curry's solution for West Virginia also became her means of staying home. During

**Pam Curry
Civic Entrepreneur
West Virginia**

the past 14 years, as the leader of CEO, Curry has helped West Virginia entrepreneurs realize their economic potential and at the same time dug her roots firmly in West Virginia.

Like Pam Curry, Beth Strube wanted to dig her roots in rural America. Her home is Dickinson, North Dakota, and her story is next.

Beth Strube
Dickinson, North Dakota
Business Entrepreneur

One minute she's editing a preschool lesson on animal ABC's. The next, she's reading *The Wall Street Journal*. Beth Strube's business serves small children and their caretakers, but running a business grossing $1 million in sales annually is not child's play. Strube is president of Funshine Express, Inc., which originates and distributes preschool curriculum. From downtown Dickinson, North Dakota, she manages 14 employees and serves a customer base of 3,000 to 4,000—an impressive increase from her start in 1995 when she had two employees, 30 customers and a copy machine in her basement.

Beth illustrates the style of so many successful entrepreneurs. She has a passion (kids) and saw a need to fulfill (better preschool curricula). She networked and acquired the skills she needed to take an evolving dream and grow it into an exceptional business. Dickinson, North Dakota (some refer to this community as North Dakota's entrepreneurial community), supported Beth. They accepted her idea for this unique business and treated her venture like a more traditional business development opportunity, making the full range of economic development resources, including financing, available to her.

Kentucky Highlands
Investment
Corporation,
Entrepreneurial
Development
Organization,
Southeastern Kentucky

Our next story is about an organization that has excelled in its support of entrepreneurs: The Kentucky Highlands Investment Corporation.

Kentucky Highlands Investment Corporation (KHIC) is based in London, Kentucky, and serves a nine-county rural region in southeastern Kentucky. This organization has been around for a long time, and it has become what we call an Entrepreneurial Support Organization (ESO). Started in 1968, KHIC serves a tough corner of rural America. Economic and social challenges run deep in this part of Appalachian Kentucky. Providing access to capital is a primary strategy KHIC employs to support area entrepreneurs. However, what makes the Corporation unique is that, over time, the organization discovered that investment capital alone was not enough. KHIC becomes every bit as involved with entrepreneurs as is required to ensure their success. In some cases, KHIC staff members join the management teams of entrepreneurial companies. The corporation is among a handful of Entrepreneurial Support Organizations that represent best practice in rural America. Other ESOs worth investigating include Northern Initiatives in Michigan, Coastal Enterprises of Maine and AceNet of Ohio.

The preceding profiles of people, businesses and organizations illustrate the diversity among entrepreneurs. All share the common motivation to create, enhancing themselves and their communities. So how do we get a handle on the entrepreneurs in our community? The following framework can provide a good start to answering this question for your community.

Lens #3 Entrepreneurial Talent Framework

If our development goal is to grow our community through entrepreneurs who create expanding businesses and stronger civic resources, we must find ways to better understand who they are and what their needs are as well. We like to use the concept of entrepreneurial or "E" talent to help communities begin this discovery process. The concept of E talent moves us beyond quibbling over "who's an entrepreneur" and gets us focused on uncovering the E talent within our communities.

We have developed a framework for identifying and organizing entrepreneurial talent within a community. It is a no nonsense approach that allows sophistication without complexity. Everyone in our community can be placed in one of five basic entrepreneurial talent categories:

- **Type 1 – Limited Potential**
- **Type 2 – Potential Entrepreneurs**
- **Type 3 – Business Owners**
- **Type 4 – Entrepreneurs**
- **Type 5 – Civic Entrepreneurs**

We'll start by focusing on the first four types of business or private entrepreneurs. We'll talk about civic entrepreneurs a little later in this chapter.

BY THE NUMBERS

Most research suggests that one in 10 American adults is actively engaged in entrepreneurship, the process of starting a business. Included in the other 90% of all adults are those with limited potential to ever become entrepreneurs along with those who may have unfulfilled entrepreneurial potential.

LIMITED POTENTIAL Dr. Tom Lyons, an expert on entrepreneurship from the University of Louisville, makes the point that entrepreneurs are made not born. The research he cites strongly suggests that any person can be entrepreneurial. While we agree with the findings of this research, we recognize that most Americans are not and are unlikely to become entrepreneurs. For example, young children, aging elders, persons unable to work or persons who would really rather be employees comprise a large category of limited potential persons. However, changing circumstances can move persons within this framework. That primary school youngster will grow up and in high school may become very entrepreneurial creating a first business venture before graduation.

POTENTIAL ENTREPRENEURS Motivation is a key ingredient essential for entrepreneurial behavior and success. Entrepreneurs must be passionate about creating and growing ventures. Within the potential entrepreneurs group there are three subgroups—youth, aspiring and start-ups. Since entrepreneurship is a learned behavior, any young person has the potential to become an entrepreneur. Youth represent a massive population of potential entrepreneurs. The question is whether we are educating and motivating young people to become employees or entrepreneurs. Aspiring entrepreneurs are those who are actively considering crossing the bridge and engaging in the entrepreneurial process. Finally, start-ups are those who have crossed the bridge from thinking about it to doing it. They are now in the first stages of the entrepreneurial process of creating and growing a venture.

Potential entrepreneurs are just that—they have the potential to be an entrepreneur. There is a motivation driving them to pursue the entrepreneurial track. The critical question here is whether they can acquire the knowledge and skills to succeed. Are they personally able to launch that first venture? Can they acquire the necessary skills quickly enough to succeed with the venture? Finally, can they acquire the comfort levels necessary to thrive in the entrepreneurial process? For most, the answer is no. However, our field research strongly suggests that in communities with active support environments, the number of potential entrepreneurs who move forward in creating successful ventures rises.

BUSINESS OWNERS   We have concluded that all persons in business have some entrepreneurial traits, but that all business owners/operators are not entrepreneurs. For many, each day they wake, open the business, run it and then go home. They are focused managers of their enterprises. However, life changes and motivations can change as well. For example, a new Wal-Mart opening 20 miles down the road, the desire to bring a family member into the business, or even the desire to break out of a rut and do more with one's life can be motivation for entrepreneurial behavior. Ewing Marion Kauffman (founder of the Kauffman Foundation) often identified the difference between a business owner and an entrepreneur in the following way: A business owner works "in" the business while an entrepreneur works "on" the business. The difference is profound. Revitalizing, growing and reinventing a business are inherently entrepreneurial.

Within the world of business owners, there are at least three subgroups— survival, lifestyle and re-start business owners. Throughout rural America there are many self-employed persons who are creatively patching multiple economic activities together to make a living. Typically, the survival ventures are not doing particularly well, but they are keeping food on the table and a home in place. Lifestyle businesses are also numerous and range from the successful family practice doctor to the corner bookstore on Main Street. Often these businesses are successful, but their owners/operators lack the motivation or capacity to grow the venture. Finally, there are the re-starts. They have tried business before and come up short, but they are trying again. There is a degree of motivation driving their new efforts, but whether they become successful entrepreneurs is yet to be determined.

ENTREPRENEURS   Our fourth group, entrepreneurs, includes those persons who have demonstrated they have the motivation and capacity to create and grow successful ventures. These are the folks who are actively evolving, inventing and creating more robust, dynamic and successful ventures (at least that is their expectation). They are not simply running their business each day—they are creating it for success tomorrow.

There are three subgroups—growth-oriented, entrepreneurial growth companies and serial entrepreneurs. Growth-oriented entrepreneurs are succeeding and are driven to grow their

BY THE NUMBERS

There are ready statistics on corporations, number of businesses, small businesses, microenterprise and self-employment. These numbers all provide part of a picture. Collecting these numbers for your community is important. Among those already engaged in business, there is huge potential for entrepreneurial development.

BY THE NUMBERS

There is little definitive data on growth-oriented entrepreneurs; however, we have found in our field research that 5% to 15% of existing businesses may fit this classification. There is good research that suggests between 4% and 5% of existing businesses fit the definition of

(continued on next page)

41

an entrepreneurial growth company (EGC). Less is known about serial entrepreneurs, but we believe the percentage of businesses that fit this definition is relatively small— maybe 1% to 2%.

A POWERFUL TOOL

With help from rural communities and economic developers throughout rural America, we have developed a tool that can help your community identify, understand and target your entrepreneurial talent. "Understanding Entrepreneurial Talent" is a useful tool, and we explore how it can help your community in Chapter 7 on Assessment.

ventures. They see new markets, profit centers or products to be created. They hold the promise of growth with the associated job creation and profits. Entrepreneurial growth companies or EGCs (sometimes referred to as gazelles) have figured it out. They represent just four to five percent of all American businesses. They are achieving sustained growth rates of 15% or more each year and are doubling in size every five years. Finally, there are serial entrepreneurs. This is a rare breed, the folks who are driven to create multiple ventures. They love the process of creating something new, but generally get bored in running the venture once it is up and going.

CIVIC ENTREPRENEURS   They share the same motivation, but they live by a different bottom line. Sometimes they are both business and civic entrepreneurs like Maxine Moul. Civic entrepreneurs create programs, institutions and resources that enrich our communities and our lives. They build wonderful children's museums, great park systems, effective public health clinics, life-saving health systems and even remarkable police departments. Sometimes, they are organized as part of government, as nonprofit organizations, informal neighborhood or community groups and civic organizations. As with business entrepreneurs, they perceive and act upon opportunities. They acquire the skills of team building, venture planning, mobilizing resources, reaching markets and creating value.

There is a powerful connection between civic entrepreneurs and entrepreneurship rates. Our field research clearly shows that communities with high rates of civic entrepreneurs are the kinds of communities that also create a high quality of life. These are the environments in which business entrepreneurs can thrive. Any community-based entrepreneurship strategy should embrace supporting civic entrepreneurship on an equal footing with business entrepreneurship.

So what does all this mean? The answer is simple. Creating a supportive environment for entrepreneurs begins with an understanding of your community's E talent. Our ability to truly energize our community's entrepreneurial talent requires different support systems for different entrepreneurs.

Entrepreneurship – What Is It?

Entrepreneurship is the complex process by which entrepreneurs envision, create and grow ventures. To understand entrepreneurship, we need to understand the necessary components of the process:

- **Creativity**
- **Innovation**
- **Motivation**
- **Capacity**

Let's explore these four concepts within the context of making your community entrepreneur friendly.

Creativity

As we described earlier in this chapter, rural economies continue to be dominated by sectors that are more strongly connected to the old economy than to the new economy. However, there are some sectors—existing, emerging, and potential—that may provide new economic development opportunities for rural communities. While some of these sectors may be familiar to you and your community, others require you to think more creatively about the opportunities they may hold for your local economy.

Creativity is defined by Webster as:

Having the ability or power to create things.
Productive.
Characterized by originality, expressiveness and imagination.

Like artists, actors, playwrights, authors, musicians, inventors, athletes and other perceived creative people, entrepreneurs are part of what Richard Florida calls the "creative class." Highly successful entrepreneurs are driven to create. Chances are their drive to create is the most powerful motivation moving them forward in the entrepreneurship process. Being creative can be both frustrating and energizing. The ability to create new things (in this case businesses or civic resources) is an incredible high. However, when the creative process is not working, entrepreneurs, like other creative people can become frustrated and challenged.

43

Most entrepreneurs are not the same folks who developed the new idea, product, services, resource or approach. Rather, they are the ones who see value in new ideas and creatively take innovation to a commercial plane. That brings us to our next important concept—innovation.

Innovation

Innovation occurs when new wealth is created and change becomes transformational. Innovation may not be high tech, life saving or even useful. Remember the "pet rock" craze? At the heart of the entrepreneurial process, entrepreneurs perceive innovation and are able to take it to market. They transform ideas into commercial products or civic services that folks want and are willing to pay for. New wealth is generally created during this process of innovation commercialization. That is why entrepreneurs and others who are part of the early commercialization phase generally become rich.

Creativity and the ability to do things with perceived innovations are foundational with entrepreneurs. However, the motivations that drive entrepreneurial behavior are wide ranging. Our next important concept in understanding entrepreneurship is motivation.

Motivation

There is a myth that equates entrepreneurship with greed. Somehow, our society believes that entrepreneurs are driven to create by money. However, like most myths, this one is largely untrue. Of course, entrepreneurs enjoy and appreciate making money, but usually money is not their most important, driving motivation.

Ray Smilor, in his landmark book *Daring Visionaries*, shares insights on this important point. In Section One of his book, Smilor talks about the soul of the entrepreneur. He employs the word "passion." If there is a common theme, this is it—All entrepreneurs do indeed have some kind a passion:

- To live the kind of life you want
- To create a service that meets a critical need
- To grow a company that employs thousands
- To prove your worth
- To make a better life for yourself and family

These examples describe very different motivations, but all reflect powerful passions. To build supportive environments in rural communities, we must take the time to understand the motivations that are driving our entrepreneurs. In doing so, we are better prepared to enable and support them.

Motivation is fundamental, but just being passionate is not enough to succeed as an entrepreneur. Acquiring the capacity is equally important. Few entrepreneurs with the capacity, but lacking motivation, succeed with their ventures. We also find few entrepreneurs who succeed with passion alone. It is clear that the individuals who realize success have strong motivation and a willingness to acquire specialized capacity. Our final key idea about entrepreneurship, then, is capacity.

Capacity

Successful entrepreneurs do not start with all the knowledge, skills and insights necessary to create thriving ventures. They acquire these skills, develop them and employ them consistently and effectively. Five core capacities enable entrepreneurial success.

ABILITY TO PERCEIVE OPPORTUNITY

First and foremost, entrepreneurs develop a heightened ability to perceive opportunities. A very successful entrepreneur will perceive more opportunities walking down a street than most of us will in a year's time. However, successful entrepreneurs also develop discipline. They become good at not only perceiving opportunities, but also assessing them and determining if there's a fit with their evolving game plan. There is a focus that prevents vision and mission drift.

ABILITY TO ASSESS AND MANAGE RISK

There is a myth that entrepreneurs are risk takers. While there may be a shred of truth to this myth, in fact entrepreneurs hate risk. They become very skilled at risk identification, assessment and management. Entrepreneurs understand that too much risk can kill an idea. The ability to effectively deal with risk distinguishes successful from less successful entrepreneurs.

(continued on next page)

ABILITY TO BUILD A TEAM

Ernesto Sirolli, the founder of *Enterprise Facilitation*™, makes the point that no individual has all the passion and skills necessary to succeed in business. He argues that to succeed, an entrepreneur must have passion and capability in the production, marketing and finances of a venture. In fact, entrepreneurs can become highly skilled at team building. They learn what kinds of team members they need and figure out how to assemble the right human resources. Great teams build great ventures.

ABILITY TO MOBILIZE RESOURCES

Another myth is that successful entrepreneurs have deep pocket venture investors. The reality is that most successful entrepreneurial growth companies start like everyone else—with too few resources and dependency upon family, friends, fools and their credit cards. Here again is an attribute that distinguishes highly successful from less successful entrepreneurs. Skilled entrepreneurs learn how to mobilize resources. They can mobilize not only necessary investment capital, but also strategic partners, people, facilities and whatever else is necessary for success.

ABILITY TO ENSURE CREATIVITY

Finally, many entrepreneurs are not happy becoming managers of successful growing companies. They hire folks like chief financial officers to ensure good management. Skilled entrepreneurs learn how to keep growing and maturing companies creative. They learn how to develop environments and processes that allow companies to recreate themselves and grow.

Successful entrepreneurs acquire many skills, but we believe these five capacities are the most important of those shared by most entrepreneurs.

Entrepreneurs Can Make the Difference

Entrepreneurs have been with us for a long time. They are a central part of American culture and identity. We take pride in our innovative ways. We respect the upstart with an idea who becomes widely successful. Entrepreneurship is more than a creative force that enriches our economies and communities. It is also a power pathway that creates opportunity and equality within America. Passion, hard work and the willingness to learn can enable ventures large and small to thrive, creating better lives for many.

Despite entrepreneurship's historic and central role within America, in many ways it has not been part of our development game plan. In rural America we have tended to focus on sustaining natural resource industries such as agriculture, timber, fisheries and energy. Today, while natural resource commodities continue to be important to many rural landscapes, it is increasingly clear that a future in the 21st century cannot be built solely on this foundation.

Since World War II, we have sought to diversify our economies beyond natural resources through industrial relocation. For 50 years, America's factories left the cities in search of cheaper land, labor and other production inputs. This strategy worked well for many communities. Industries, investment and jobs flowed to thousands of rural communities and contributed to their development. However, like natural resources, the future of our rural communities cannot rely on business relocation to give them purpose and economic meaning. Today, the greener pasture for many of these factories is China, Mexico or other places where land, labor and production costs are even lower.

Rural communities are seeking new development strategies. Don Betts, with Georgia Tech's Economic Development Institute, talks about the importance of entrepreneurship as the bedrock of a rural development strategy. Creating a community environment that supports entrepreneurs also creates a place that is attractive to new industry locations and where people want to stay and grow their businesses. Entrepreneurship is now on the rural development radar screen of many rural regions. However, a major challenge remains to make the case that entrepreneurship can

(Five Myths continued)

competencies. Fourth, most entrepreneurs do not have a fully sorted out vision of their enterprise. They get started and evolve based on a good concept and great team. Finally, venture capital is not terribly important (except in certain sectors such as drugs and biotechnology) to emergent companies. Early ventures are financed by the three Fs—family, friends and fools (primarily credit card companies and suppliers).

In the final analysis, we are talking about one in 10 Americans (probably fewer in rural America) who have the motivation and can acquire the capacity to create and grow an enterprise. A very small group of very special people achieve the capacity and opportunity to create a high growth enterprise—only four to five in 100 enterprises.

National Commission on Entrepreneurship. Five Myths About Entrepreneurs: Understanding How Businesses Start and Grow.

lead to meaningful economic development. In Chapter Five, we explore the emerging rationale supporting entrepreneurship as a core rural development strategy in the 21st century.

Additional Resources

More information is available on the *E²* *Energizing Entrepreneurs* website, www.energizingentrepreneurs.org. Once there, click on "Entrepreneurs and Entrepreneurship" to find resources that support the information in this chapter.

We recommend the following five resources as a great place to expand your understanding of entrepreneurs:

First, we recommend Ray Smilor's book, *Daring Visionaries: How Entrepreneurs Build Companies, Inspire Allegiance, and Create Wealth*. This is an easy read. Smilor provides fantastic insight about who entrepreneurs are and what motivates them to create. Adams Media Corporation.

Second, we recommend a series of short reports published by the National Commission on Entrepreneurship. These reports can be found at www.ruraleship.org, offering a quick and well-rounded view of entrepreneurs.

Third, there is the classic that is a must read for all who want a deeper understanding—Michael Gerber's *The E Myth Revisited*. Gerber provides great insight into the heart and soul of entrepreneurs and entrepreneurship in America. HarperCollins Books.

Fourth, a controversial but worthy read is Richard Florida's book *The Rise of the Creative Class*. This book does not focus squarely on entrepreneurs, but entrepreneurs are part of the creative class Dr. Florida explores in this book. Basic Books.

Finally, Amar Bhide's book, *The Origin and Evolution of New Businesses*, will challenge you and take you further into the entrepreneurial process. Oxford University Press.

CHAPTER 5
MAKING THE CASE—
WHY ENTREPRENEURSHIP?

The Challenge of Embracing Entrepreneurship

Economic development practitioners are struggling to find strategies that can bring hope to their rural communities—strategies that offer the promise of new jobs, more income, and increased wealth and capacity in rural hometowns across the country. As we've traveled the country, talking with leaders in communities and states, we find economic development practitioners struggling with an important question. How can they make the case in their communities that supporting entrepreneurs is the key to improving economic development prospects for the future?

Entrepreneurs and entrepreneurship are high profile topics nationally these days. Politicians frequently mention entrepreneurs in discussions about the economy. New national entrepreneurship initiatives are being created. The entrepreneurial culture is celebrated on reality TV. However, there's a difference between talking about the importance of entrepreneurship and investing in a strategy for supporting entrepreneurs in your community or state.

Why is it so tough to embrace an entrepreneurship development strategy? Our field experience yields these suggestions:

- Economic development practitioners are reluctant to abandon the traditional tools of their trade: development of natural resources, industrial attraction and small business

IN THIS CHAPTER

> The Challenge of Embracing Entrepreneurship

> Why Entrepreneurship?

> Strategies for Making the Case

retention and expansion. These tools worked in the past and, absent a new toolkit, we tend to continue with the same, familiar strategies.

- Practitioners can find institutional support for these traditional strategies (for example, state department of commerce resources), while embracing entrepreneurship often means "going it alone." While some entrepreneurs enjoy being "lone eagles," community leaders and practitioners need support and partners as they develop new ways to find and nurture entrepreneurs.

- Community leaders are familiar with the research on traditional strategies (such as what factors give a community an advantage in attracting industry) while they know much less about research on the importance of entrepreneurship. Without this knowledge base, it's harder to figure out what needs to be done in your community to encourage entrepreneurship.

- The outcomes of investing in entrepreneurship occur over the long-term, and individual successes often don't lend themselves to public ribbon cuttings. Helping an artisan tap new regional markets via the Internet may increase sales and establish a successful business, but it can't compete with the headlines resulting from a branch plant opening.

- Until recently, we haven't had concrete examples of community and state entrepreneurship strategies that could serve as guides to others interested in supporting entrepreneurs. Embracing entrepreneurship often resulted in community leaders and economic development practitioners asking, "OK, now what do I do?" This book provides concrete answers to this fundamental question.

In spite of these challenges, community leaders, economic development practitioners and state leaders are beginning to embrace entrepreneurship as a core economic development strategy. The overwhelming response to the W.K. Kellogg Foundation's Entrepreneurship Development Systems for Rural America initiative is testimony to the burgeoning commitment to entrepreneurship across rural America. Our team is tracking initiatives in many states and regions—some championed by the private sector, others by nonprofit organizations, and others by state institutions.

In many of these rural places, community leaders have embraced the case for entrepreneurship and are developing and implementing strategies to make this case a reality. In other places, however, rural leaders need help articulating the case in a way that can garner support within the community and from state policy makers. We turn now to what the research tells us about the contribution and importance of entrepreneurship to economic development.

Why Entrepreneurship?

Community leaders who embrace entrepreneurship follow one of two approaches to make the case for entrepreneurship— one positive and one negative. The positive approach centers on the important contribution of entrepreneurs and their ventures in building stronger economies and communities. The negative approach argues that the traditional economic development strategies aren't getting the job done now, leaving the door open for new alternatives. Let's explore each of these approaches in turn, starting with the negative.

Failure of Traditional Economic Development Strategies

Rural communities have traditionally focused their economic development activities in three areas: natural resource development, industrial attraction and small business development. With some exceptions, notably in high amenity rural places and in rural areas adjacent to cities, these strategies are not leading to the creation of sustainable rural economies. While the explanation for this failure differs, the result is the same for the rural communities left behind:

- NATURAL RESOURCE DEVELOPMENT   The traditional natural resource industries (i.e., farming, mining, forestry, fisheries and energy) have experienced significant industrialization and consolidation over the past 50 years. The result is fewer farms, mines, lumber and energy companies coupled with decision making concentrated in ownership outside the local communities. Policy changes and global competition have created an environment where it is tougher for small, entrepreneurial farms and natural resource companies to be successful. For example, many North Carolina communities are being forced to reinvent themselves, as tobacco farming and the industries that support it undergo significant downsizing.

- INDUSTRIAL ATTRACTION Rural communities benefited from the relocation decisions of branch plants over the past several decades—attracting footloose plants in search of cheaper land and labor and business-friendly environments. However, the reality today is much different than in the past. Cheaper land and labor are found not in rural America but in the emerging economies of China, India and Mexico. Shuttered factories have become a reality in rural America. David Birch, a pioneer in drawing attention to the important contribution of smaller enterprises to economic growth in the U.S., notes that only about 1% of new jobs are coming from relocations. The odds are against any particular rural community attracting the next major automobile or pharmaceutical plant.

- SMALL BUSINESS DEVELOPMENT In the past, rural communities captured the income generated in their local economies through farms and industry by developing a vibrant local business sector that met the needs of residents in the community. Downtown merchants provided the retail goods that consumers demanded while local businesses supplied inputs to farmers and manufacturers alike. However, pressure has been put on local businesses from the increasing competition of big box retailers, the Internet and industry-supplier relationships dictated from outside the local area. Empty stores along Main Street are as much a feature of rural communities as abandoned factories and empty industrial parks.

Failure can often lead to despair—an urge to pack up the bags and head to greener pastures. However, failure can also lead to innovation—a willingness to try a new approach to creating a vibrant, sustainable rural economy. For many, that new approach is entrepreneurship and, as we'll see now, there is a growing body of evidence about the positive contribution of entrepreneurship to building strong economies.

Contribution of Entrepreneurship to Economic Development

Twenty-five years ago, David Birch first shined a spotlight on the small business sector in his book, *The Job Creation Process*. Birch showed that small businesses created most of the new jobs in our economy, putting entrepreneurs and entrepreneurship center stage. More recently, the Global Entrepreneurship Monitor project has provided us with the best picture of the contribution of entrepreneurs to economic growth in the U.S. and other countries. We now have five years worth of insights gained from this cross-national study. The project presents key findings:

- There is a strong *positive* relationship between the level of entrepreneurial activity in a country and economic growth. Up to 70% of the difference in rates of economic growth across countries can be attributed to entrepreneurial activity.
- No countries with *high* levels of entrepreneurial activity experienced low levels of economic growth. Very few countries build robust economies without strong entrepreneurial activity. Entrepreneurs and the businesses they create contribute to strong economies in their home countries.

Work by the National Commission on Entrepreneurship, *Embracing Innovation: Entrepreneurship and American Economic Growth*, confirms the importance of entrepreneurs to economic vitality:

- Small entrepreneurs are responsible for 67% of inventions and 95% of radical innovations in the U.S. since World War II. Such diverse products as frozen foods, air conditioning, the cotton picker and the helicopter resulted from the drive and innovation of small entrepreneurs.
- A small group of high growth entrepreneurs, only 5% to 15% of all firms, created about two thirds of net new jobs in the late 1990s. In many parts of the country, these small entrepreneurial firms are contributing new jobs at the same time as larger firms are cutting back employment.

• Through their innovation and creativity, entrepreneurs are transforming existing business sectors (think Cabela's for hunting and fishing equipment) and creating new sectors (think biotech) that are competitive throughout the world.

While much of this research focuses on the role of entrepreneurs in national economies, a groundbreaking national, multi-year study, the Panel Study of Entrepreneurial Dynamics, found that entrepreneurship is widespread in the U.S. across all racial and ethnic groups. At any given time, about 10 million adults are trying to create a new business. While entrepreneurs are everywhere, urban areas boast higher rates of entrepreneurship than rural communities.

Rural geography, however, doesn't have to be a limiting factor for entrepreneurs. Focusing on entrepreneurial growth companies (EGCs), the National Commission on Entrepreneurship found that EGCs were located in every region in the country. In *High Growth Companies: Mapping America's Entrepreneurial Landscape*, the commission shows that in 1997 at least one high growth firm was located in almost every county in the U.S. A study for the W. K. Kellogg Foundation by the Corporation for Enterprise Development, *Mapping Rural Entrepreneurship*, identified entrepreneurial places and programs throughout rural America. In addition, our fieldwork has identified remarkable entrepreneurial communities across rural America, such as Kearney, Nebraska; Fairfield, Iowa; and Appalachian Kentucky.

Putting all these facts and figures together suggests that entrepreneurs are a vital part of our economy, contributing jobs and innovation to communities and regions across the country. This body of research has captured the attention of policy makers and leaders in a variety of settings—from the Georgia statehouse to the Kansas legislature; from foundation boardrooms to the National Governors Association. However, how can you use this information to make the case for entrepreneurship in your rural community?

Strategies for Making the Case in Your Community

Making the case in your community requires a leap of faith. Whether you are persuaded by the evidence linking entrepreneurship to economic prosperity or whether you are ready to try anything that might reverse the downward spiral in your community, the first step requires making a commitment to really understand what entrepreneurship development is all about. This understanding occurs at two different levels.

At one level, you can access the resources that give you a "big picture" understanding of the role of entrepreneurs in economic development. Some of the best resources are included at the end of this chapter. These resources can provide the context for your community to begin to embrace entrepreneurship as a core development strategy.

At a second level, you can begin to dig in and learn what other communities and places are doing to create environments that support entrepreneurs. For some of these places, such as Fairfield, Iowa, and Kearney, Nebraska, there are stories that describe what they are doing and how they developed their strategies. The web site of the RUPRI Center for Rural Entrepreneurship (www.ruraleship.org) is a good place to start your learning process.

You might also decide to visit communities in your region that are actively engaged in entrepreneurship development. There's no substitute for learning from people we call the early adopters or innovators in this field. You can ask the tough questions: Why are you pursuing entrepreneurship development in your community? What is your strategy? How did you gain community support for this strategy? How is it working?

With this deeper understanding of entrepreneurship, you can begin to consider what your community needs to do to embark on this new approach to economic development. Armed with good data and stories of how other communities are making entrepreneurship work, you will be able to energize others in your community in support of a new strategy.

You can start with the usual suspects—those organizations in your community that are already working with the business com-

E² ENERGIZING ENTREPRENEURSHIP IN RURAL AMERICA– A TRAINING PROGRAM PRACTITIONERS

Early on, our team understood that making the case for entrepreneurship in communities often means providing community leaders with new economic development tools. We developed a training program to give economic development for practitioners and other community leaders the tools they need to make an effective case for entrepreneurship and to develop a strategy appropriate to each community. The program has been shared with hundreds of individuals across the country, in a variety of formats. Participating in an E² academy often helps frame the issues for community leaders and is useful for getting a leadership team " on the same page" in terms of entrepreneurship as a core development strategy. If you think an E² academy might be useful in your community, contact us to learn more about upcoming training opportunities.

munity. Visit with staff at the local chamber of commerce, the small business development center in your region, a local community college, and private sector service providers such as attorneys, accountants and bankers. You can share with them what you've learned about entrepreneurship, specifically what is happening in other rural places across the country.

Through these initial conversations, you'll find the leaders in your community who are most interested in an entrepreneurship strategy. These leaders, in turn, become the core of a community steering committee that makes the case for entrepreneurship to the broader community. At this point, you are positioned to begin considering the strategies that might work best in your community. Let the journey begin!

Additional Resources

For more information visit the E^2 *Energizing Entrepreneurs* website at www.energizingentrepreneurs.org. Once there, click on "Making the Case" to find resources that support the information in this chapter.

To develop the "big picture" understanding of the role of entrepreneurs and the businesses they create in economic development, we suggest the following:

The Global Entrepreneurship Monitor Project Reports. These reports are available for 1999-2003. The best place to start is with the Executive Report for a specific year. All publications, including specific country reports, are available at www.gemconsortium.org.

Several publications from the National Commission on Entrepreneurship provide good background information on entrepreneurship. The following three publications are available at http://www.publicforuminstitute.org/nde/reports/index.htm:
- *Entrepreneurship: A Candidate's Guide*
- *High-Growth Companies: Mapping America's Entrepreneurial Landscape*
- *Embracing Innovation: Entrepreneurship and American Economic Growth*

The Entrepreneur Next Door: Characteristics of Individuals Starting Companies in America provides great information on who in this country is actively engaged in starting a company. The report is available at www.ruraleship.org.

To learn more about the people and places actively engaged in entrepreneurship development, you can start by looking at some of the stories we have collected. Our library has case studies of organizations and regions pursuing entrepreneurship along with stories of organizations, communities, and individual entrepreneurs, both private and social. Start your search at www.ruraleship.org. If you want more information, your next stop is with the individuals and communities themselves.

Chapter 6
Readiness for Economic Development and Entrepreneurship

A Community Success Story

Ord, Nebraska, in rural Valley County, is not unlike many rural communities around the country. It has been losing youth to out-migration. The town's population is shrinking and the percentage of older citizens is increasing. The community runs the risk of losing vast quantities of owned assets as they are transferred to members of the next generation, most of whom live outside the community. Other concerns include employment and under-employment, workforce development, lack of industry, government as a primary employer, and lack of amenities for both tourists and retirees.

The people of Ord and Valley County (pop. 4,647) love their community and believe in its future. Determination, good intentions, and money, however, are not enough to turn around decades of decline. Leaders in Ord realized they needed help to identify how best to use limited resources for the most strategic outcomes. They invited the Nebraska Community Foundation, the RUPRI Center for Rural Entrepreneurship, and the Heartland Center for Leadership Development to become part of their team.

The first activity in Valley County was the development of the Valley County Foundation, formed to accept a bequest of $1.2 million. The first grants from this donation were made in May 2000, attracting a great deal of community attention to the idea of local giving and the potential impact of wealth transfer.

During 2001, the Valley County Foundation received additional gifts and expectancies partially in response to two training events with financial planners and an endowment-building workshop.

In November 2000, local leaders worked hard to pass a local option sales tax that generates $250,000 per year for community improvement and community economic development. Their first action was to hire an economic development specialist/chamber director. They also adopted an extensive strategic plan with an emphasis on industrial recruitment. Difficulties with implementing this plan led them to seek other options.

In 2002, the Valley County Economic Development Council (VCEDC) began a partnership with the Heartland Center for Leadership Development, the Nebraska Community Foundation and the RUPRI Center for Rural Entrepreneurship. Together, these organizations launched a pilot project called "HomeTown Competitiveness." In August of 2002, the partners worked with community leaders to evaluate the existing economic development plan, which consisted of more than 20 goals. Two goals were identified as priorities: facilitate small business transfer and assist potential breakout entrepreneurs. In addition, the group worked on goals for wealth transfer and community capacity building.

Also in August of 2002, the group began its Leadership Quest (LQ) program. The LQ program brought new energy and new leadership to the task of creating a sustainable and healthy community in Valley County. Workshops, group activities and class work helped participants learn new things about themselves and their community, develop and practice new skills, and recommit to building a better community. LQ has done more than develop the skills and talents of participants. More people in the community are volunteering to run for office, to serve on local boards, and to help with local projects. The Leadership Committee now offers the program yearly and orchestrates alumni reunions to keep the spirit of helping alive.

In September of 2002, the business development committee conducted business visitations and, as a result, they agreed to target specific businesses interested in growing. In addition, they found that a number of Main Street businesses were struggling with business transfer. During the following year, local leaders and economic development specialists began working with these owners to devise new strategies and options.

This project already shows great promise and, since its inception, the community has celebrated several successes:

Valley County has exceeded its goal of capturing 5% of its predicted inter-generational transfer of wealth. It now has $6.7 million in charitable contributions and expectancies to support and sustain community and economic development.

Local banks are providing adult scholarships to a business boot camp, and 15 new business owners will sharpen their skills through the Nebraska EDGE program. Elementary students meet once a week to develop prototype products and services, write business plans, and apply for real loans from real local bankers.

In three years Leadership Quest has graduated 70 youths and adults. A wealthy alum living in Arizona flies in to teach a class on growing entrepreneurs.

A young adult returned home to start an irrigation well business and another plans a local dental practice. Outside investors are renovating vacant buildings.

Even though Valley County is comparatively poor, residents are beginning to embrace asset-based economic development strategies. A one-cent local sales tax has created a fund that has made seven small business loans.

Numerous small businesses and entrepreneurs have been evaluated, and several of these businesses are ready to grow, prosper and generate new wealth.

These collective efforts are beginning to create positive momentum and attitude shift about the future prospects of living and prospering in Ord and Valley County.

Readiness Framework for Entrepreneurship Development

As the story of Ord shows, communities must evaluate readiness in two ways:
- Are we ready for economic development?
- Are we ready for entrepreneurship development?

The folks in Ord made a commitment of time, talent and

treasure to the economic development process, ultimately hiring their first economic development staff person. Once their readiness for economic development was demonstrated, it was time to turn to the next issue—are we ready for entrepreneurship?

Entrepreneurship development is more than just building businesses in your community. It is also about establishing an entrepreneurial culture. It requires revisiting the "can-do" pioneer spirit of many rural towns and overcoming challenges and obstacles that may be encountered along the way.

Our experience has shown that communities are "ready" to engage in entrepreneurship development when certain qualities and characteristics are evident:

• Particular capacities in human, financial, and physical infrastructure

The schools in Edcouch and Elsa, near the Mexican border in eastern Texas, have shown great success in using grants, youth involvement and organizational development to build capacity in this area.

• A supportive business/entrepreneurial history

Farmington, Missouri, offers a collaborative group of organizations, such as the chamber, the economic development organization and regional councils, to support new business development.

• A strong self-image with positive citizen and community attitudes

Watsonville, California, is a good example of an ethnically diverse community working hard to maintain citizen involvement and a positive image.

• Open and creative community leadership, or leadership environment, that encourages and nurtures emerging leaders

Hobbs, New Mexico, used a leadership project to bring new and diverse populations into leadership roles.

You can arrive at a better understanding of your community's readiness level by exploring each of these elements.

Infrastructure

When we think of infrastructure, we usually focus on our community's physical plant—roads, buildings and utilities. However, for entrepreneurship development, you need to think more broadly, including human and financial resources.

HUMAN INFRASTRUCTURE   Citizens of successful communities take pride in their communities and are civic-minded and involved, as demonstrated through festivals and celebrations. They are taking action to make the community a better place to live, work and play. There is an atmosphere of "family," with an air of inclusiveness that includes the newcomer as well as the old-timer. These communities are accepting of entrepreneurs who may walk to the beat of a slightly different drummer!

Communities that are ready to pursue entrepreneurship development also have existing organizations that play an important role in the life of the community. Communities that have survived over time and are vital and vibrant have civic and service clubs, churches and their respective organizations, and a number of other groups. These groups provide valuable rosters of active community members and give evidence of a community's willingness to work together, achieve and succeed. Many of these organizations may already be committed to supporting and nurturing entrepreneurs—they get it!

A community that is "ready" also displays an attitude of nurturing its citizens. Communities that are ready for economic development and entrepreneurship programs encourage flexibility and creativity in meeting new challenges and by so doing, tend to attract further resources and opportunities. These communities are able to retain their youth, or even attract new young people to move to town, stemming population decline. Communities that educate themselves about entrepreneurship and are willing to create an entrepreneurial culture not only attract entrepreneurial people, but frequently "grow" their own hometown entrepreneurs.

FINANCIAL INFRASTRUCTURE   Communities that are ready for entrepreneurship development have an understanding of, and willingness to, invest. Remember our "rural community as corporation" example from Chapter 2? A rural community with 5,000 residents will likely generate a $750 million economy. If your community were a $750 million company, how much would you invest annually to ensure your competitiveness? While some rural community programs can run on volunteers, successful entrepreneurship development programs need staff and dollars to support services and programs. By the same token, our research has shown that frugality is a way of life in successful small communities and expenditures are made carefully. People aren't afraid to spend money when they believe they should. But neither are they spendthrifts. Expenditures are often seen as investments in the future of the community.

Financial capacity or the ability to find financing in communities is a vital component to an entrepreneurship development program. When a community is ready for such a program, flexibility or creativity in financing is evident, with the creation of non-traditional forms such as economic development funds or loan pools.

In addition to monetary resources, communities that are "ready" have existing and experienced business owners. They also attract individuals such as attorneys, accountants, and insurance and marketing professionals. Resource people from local or regional development boards and similar organizations are identified and utilized. Such communities usually have an active chamber of commerce.

PHYSICAL INFRASTRUCTURE The ready community takes into consideration its physical infrastructure as it begins to create an entrepreneurship development program. Traditional infrastructure, such as streets and sidewalks, water systems and sewage facilities, is important to maintain and improve. It is a fundamental necessity for any community. A community that is strapped with outdated, poorly functioning, or inadequately built infrastructure will find itself unattractive to the potential entrepreneur. Aging infrastructure is costly and may price your town out of the entrepreneur's interest or ability to pay.

However, it is equally important that a community expands its concept of infrastructure, particularly as you engage in entrepreneurship development. In today's economy, your community must consider citizens' (and entrepreneurs') desire for particular services and amenities, such as high-speed access to the Internet. Does the community, through local government or other organizations, have a web presence? Can people find a community's businesses on the web? Douglas, Wyoming is a great example of a rural community that focuses on the need to be a truly "wired" community.

These are all "livability" factors that a community needs to consider. Design and planning for future development and growth should consider the needs of growing businesses. In addition, the built environment plays an important role in attracting and retaining individuals. A beautifully restored downtown, common sense traffic gateways, cherished coffee shops or libraries, and ample recreational opportunities are some of the amenities that provide space for social and economic gatherings. Good design can help create space where entrepreneurial ideas are hatched and worked out.

Community History, Self-Image and Attitude

Many rural communities were founded on, and still rely on, a deep sense of the pioneer spirit. Our experience shows that parallels exist between this deep pioneer identification and a community developing an entrepreneurial strategy. A pioneer spirit can be a valuable tool in entrepreneurship development with its "can-do" sensibility and its sense of self-reliance tempered with the necessity of creatively finding needed resources. For example, in northwestern North Dakota, eight counties and the Three Affiliated Tribes of the Fort Berthold Indian Reservation incorporated the area's pioneer history as an important value in developing the area's collaborative strategic plan.

In this vein, the pioneer spirit is rethought and revived in a community's ongoing commitment to investment in entrepreneurial efforts. Local entrepreneurs can find the assistance they need locally, from a business start-up fund, for example, and not search for capital outside of the region. When the entrepreneur succeeds, the investment remains in the community and helps fund the next entrepreneurial effort.

In addition, the "ready" community has some history of striving to develop its economic base. There is evidence of past community efforts to encourage business development. Some possibilities are business networks, mentoring programs, business incubators and/or training, counseling services, or other similar programs.

The "ready" community displays particular mindsets, or a willingness to learn new mindsets and attitudes. For example, if the community is open to exploring entrepreneurship as an economic development strategy, it must also be ready to consider what that program will require. The community must be open to making a commitment and making the decisions needed to begin the process. Central to such a commitment is the firm belief that within your community there are entrepreneurs who can create a new generation of successful businesses and that there are service providers and community leaders willing to help them achieve success.

In an era of scarce resources, entrepreneurship development also requires that your community be open to *collaboration*. Many communities will not have all the resources they need locally to support entrepreneurs or engage in another economic development activity. Is your community willing to create partnerships with other area communities to find the human and financial resources necessary to be in the economic development game? There's little reluctance in successful rural communities to seek outside help, and many of them demonstrate their success at competing for government grants and contracts for economic development, sewer and water systems, recreation, street and sidewalk improvement, and senior citizen programs.

Although outside help is sought when appropriate, it is nevertheless true that thriving small communities believe their destiny is in their own hands. Successful entrepreneurial communities are neither sitting back waiting to die nor are they sitting around waiting to be saved. Instead, they are making or growing their own economic futures. Making their communities good places to live for a long time to come is a proactive assignment, and they willingly accept it.

Community Leadership

A community ready to embark on an entrepreneurship development program is able to create a team committed to an entrepreneurship strategy. Community leaders today play a different role than they have in the past:

- They help their community through processes open to citizen participation. They *articulate* and then *communicate* a vision for entrepreneurship that most citizens can embrace with enthusiasm.
- They match community *needs* with available community skills and accessible internal and external *resources*.
- They develop *realistic strategies* that can be undertaken

today to move the community in the direction it must go to transform today's vision of an entrepreneurial community into tomorrow's reality.

Finally, the community and its leadership should realize that leaders are made, not born. That means that leadership can be learned. A "ready" community seeks out and nurtures new, emergent leaders including entrepreneurs. One of the signs of a healthy and vital community is a leadership group that recognizes the need to recruit new members into leadership roles. Because of their visibility, current leaders are in an excellent position to draw new leaders into community activity. By sharing responsibilities, current leaders can recruit and train newcomers to the leadership pool.

There are, of course, other ways to nurture new leaders, including mentoring, coaching or leadership classes. In Oregon, the Ford Family Foundation uses a multi-session statewide leadership program for rural towns designed by the Heartland Center for Leadership Development. Emerging leaders are identified for and recruited into voluntary community roles, mentored through volunteer experiences and given guidance through coaching. Coaching generally involves taking time to help the emerging leaders reflect on what they are learning and what assistance they need to make the most of their voluntary service. This coaching process is particularly important for entrepreneurs who may be new to assuming leadership roles outside of their business. What's important here is that existing leaders value and welcome new leaders as well as provide a number of ways in which people can participate in the process.

Overcoming Obstacles

In spite of the best planning, communities will encounter obstacles as they move forward with any economic development activity. Communities that are ready to embark on an entrepreneurship development program are cognizant of and have dealt with these obstacles and pitfalls. They have worked their way through them and have in place the people or mechanisms necessary to ensure action. Here are some obstacles you should be watching for:

- Leadership is controlled by a group of elites who maintain their roles by excluding others. You should strive to have many stakeholders involved in the leadership of your entrepreneurship development efforts.

- Strong individuals derail efforts by not working within a sense of community or leaders succumb to group think (a path of least resistance or conflict) or brute think (being bulldozed into accepting a solution just to be done with it). You should encourage debate and discussion from all stakeholders, keeping the community's goals in the forefront at all times.
- The decision-making process becomes mired or twisted, leading to the community choosing the wrong path or strategy. You should establish decision-making criteria and stick to them—alternatives are presented, all voices are heard, and you allow adequate time for decision-making.
- Too many approaches or steps are included, overwhelming volunteers and threatening implementation. The process with the fewest steps is the best.
- People fail to take action and the process simply dies. You should develop and commit to implementation plans that include who's responsible for seeing that actions occur.

Tools for Readiness Assessment

Remember, a community that is "ready" for entrepreneurship development has made a commitment to economic development generally and has assessed its readiness in terms of these qualities and characteristics:

- Particular capacities in human, financial, and physical infrastructure
- A supportive business/entrepreneurial history
- A strong self-image with positive citizen and community attitudes
- Open and creative community leadership, or leadership environment, that encourages and nurtures emerging leaders

What tools can you use to assess your community's readiness for entrepreneurship development? While there are many tools to assess readiness three tools are presented here: **20 Clues to Rural Community Survival, Community Readiness Factors**, and the **Rural Community Entrepreneurship Survey**. We also suggest ways in which you might want to use them in your community.

Tool 1 – 20 Clues to Rural Community Survival

The following is a list of 20 characteristics found among thriving communities, based on research conducted by the Heartland Center for Leadership Development. The Heartland Center found that thriving communities tend to possess a variety of these characteristics, but not all 20 characteristics. Review these characteristics. Based on your community, rate each characteristic as a strength (+), a weakness (-), or as neutral (/).

TOOLS FOR READINESS ASSESSMENT

TOOL 1

Community Strengths and Weaknesses

1.	Evidence of community pride	+	−	/
2.	Emphasis on quality in business and community life	+	−	/
3.	Willingness to invest in the future	+	−	/
4.	Participatory approach to community decision-making	+	−	/
5.	Cooperative community spirit	+	−	/
6.	Realistic appraisal of future opportunities	+	−	/
7.	Awareness of competitive positioning	+	−	/
8.	Knowledge of the physical environment	+	−	/
9.	Active economic development program	+	−	/
10.	Deliberate transition of power to a younger generation of leaders	+	−	/
11.	Acceptance of women in leadership roles	+	−	/
12.	Strong belief in and support of education	+	−	/
13.	Problem-solving approach to providing health care	+	−	/
14.	Strong multi-generational family orientation	+	−	/
15.	Strong presence of traditional institutions that are integral to community life	+	−	/
16.	Sound and well-maintained infrastructure	+	−	/
17.	Careful use of fiscal resources	+	−	/
18.	Sophisticated use of information resources	+	−	/
19.	Willingness to seek help from the outside	+	−	/
20.	Conviction that, in the long run, you have to do it yourself	+	−	/

**TOOLS FOR
READINESS
ASSESSMENT**

TOOL 1
(continued)

Using Tool 1 to Assess Readiness

A good way to use this tool is to bring together a diverse group of community citizens, including entrepreneurs, and have them complete the survey. Tabulate the results for the group so that you can identify areas where there is strong agreement about strengths and weaknesses, as well as those areas where some group within the community feels very strongly about certain characteristics. Alternatively, you can use this tool in several settings to get the perspectives of different groups within the community. For example, you might get the perspective of teachers by using the survey in a high school staff meeting or the perspective of local business leaders by using the survey at a chamber meeting.

Below, the Clues have been organized into six broad categories or capacities. By transferring the ratings from your survey work, you can begin to develop a broader picture of your community's strengths and weaknesses. From these findings, you can determine what strengths to accentuate and those weaknesses that require further targeting and development.

Capacity	Characteristics	Rating
Strong Local Economy	2. Emphasis on quality in business and community life 7. Awareness of competitive positioning 9. Active economic development program 17. Careful use of fiscal resources	
Natural Resources/ Infrastructure	8. Knowledge of the physical environment 16. Sound and well-maintained infrastructure 18. Sophisticated use of information resources	
Identity and Image	1. Evidence of community pride 5. Cooperative community spirit 20. Conviction that, in the long run, you have to do it yourself	
Shared Leadership	4. Participatory approach to community decision-making 10. Deliberate transition of power to a younger generation of leaders 11. Acceptance of women in leadership roles	
Support Systems	12. Strong belief in and support of education 13. Problem-solving approach to providing health care 14. Strong multi-generational family orientation 15. Strong presence of traditional institutions that are integral to community life	
Strategic Agenda	3. Willingness to invest in the future 6. Realistic appraisal of future opportunities 19. Willingness to seek help from the outside	

Tool 2 – Community Readiness Factors

Entrepreneurs do not operate in a vacuum. Their success depends to some extent on the community environment that may support, or in some cases, hinder their ability to grow and prosper. Your community's first step in implementing an entrepreneurship program is to assess how well the community currently supports its entrepreneurs. Through field-work sponsored by the RUPRI Center for Rural Entrepreneurship, we have identified six readiness factors that can determine whether a community can build a successful entrepreneurship-based economic development program.

TOOLS FOR READINESS ASSESSMENT

TOOL 2

The six readiness factors:

OPENNESS TO ENTREPRENEURSHIP Is the community open to exploring entrepreneurship as an economic development strategy? Central to such a commitment is the firm belief that within your community there are entrepreneurs who can create a new generation of successful businesses and there are service providers and community leaders willing to help them achieve success.

BALANCING BUSINESS ATTRACTION Does the community balance a traditional economic development approach with a focus on local businesses and on energizing entrepreneurs to create and build homegrown enterprises? For 50 years the mainstay economic development strategy has been business attraction, particularly the search for industries. Supporting entrepreneurship requires a willingness to broaden the economic development strategy beyond the traditional recruitment model.

ENTREPRENEURSHIP PROGRAMS Has your community had experience with entrepreneurship programs already? Check any of the following entrepreneurial programs that your community has experience with, either currently or in the past:

[　] Networking infrastructure for entrepreneurs
[　] Mentoring programs for entrepreneurs
[　] Efforts to improve business services for entrepreneurs
[　] Micro lending or other business financing services
[　] Entrepreneurial training programs such as "how to start a business" seminars or courses
[　] Business counseling services
[　] Youth entrepreneurship education programs
[　] Other programs specific to your community

(continued on next page)

TOOLS FOR READINESS ASSESSMENT

TOOL 2
(continued)

WILLINGNESS TO INVEST Most rural communities have limited experience with entrepreneurial programs. So do not assume you cannot create an entrepreneurial development strategy if your experience with these kinds of programs is limited. What is most important is a willingness to develop and support these kinds of activities.

LEADERSHIP TEAM Can your community create a team that will work on an entrepreneurial strategy? To be successful, a community needs a core leadership team committed to building and supporting an entrepreneurship program. Remember, as Margaret Mead once said, *"Never forget that a small group of thoughtful, committed citizens can change the world. Indeed it's the only thing that ever has."*

BEYOND TOWN BORDERS Is your community willing to create partnerships with other area communities to find the human and financial resources in order to be in the economic development game? We in rural America love our small towns. We value places where we know our neighbors. But in today's competitive world, we must collaborate to create enough scale and capacity to support effective economic development strategies.

Ranking Your Community's Readiness Factors

Based on your understanding of the above Community Readiness Factors, you can rank your community on each readiness factor using a 1–5 scale, where 1 is a limited degree of readiness and 5 is a high degree of readiness. This exercise is useful in terms of identifying areas that may need to be strengthened as your community pursues an entrepreneurship development strategy.

Score Card:	Not Ready			Very Ready	
Factor 1 - Openness to Entrepreneurship	1	2	3	4	5
Factor 2 - Balancing Business Attraction	1	2	3	4	5
Factor 3 - Entrepreneurship Programs	1	2	3	4	5
Factor 4 - Willingness to Invest	1	2	3	4	5
Factor 5 - Leadership Team	1	2	3	4	5
Factor 6 - Beyond Town Borders	1	2	3	4	5

Overall Score _____ (circle and sum)

Understanding the Score

1-6	Weak Score – Little Readiness – Capacity Building Required
7-12	Soft Score – Some Readiness – Gap Filling Necessary
13-18	Good Score – Readiness Potential – Begin to Build on Assets
19-24	Strong Score – Readiness Present – Build on Assets
25-30	Very Strong Score – Considerable Readiness – Energize Your Entrepreneurs

Using Tool 2 to Assess Readiness

As with Tool 1, you can address these readiness factors as part of a focus group of community leaders and residents who have an interest in entrepreneurship. It is important to bring a diverse group of leaders together so that you get different perspectives on readiness. Service providers in your community, such as a business counselor with SCORE (Service Corps of Retired Executives) or the chamber president, may have very different views on the community's readiness for entrepreneurship development than the entrepreneurs themselves. Experienced entrepreneurs may view the community environment in a different way than do new start-up entrepreneurs. You should strive to get as many different views on your community's readiness as possible.

Once you've tabulated your readiness scores, you can use this information in two ways. The overall score can help give you and others in the community a sense of the starting point—Are we in a strong position as we begin to encourage entrepreneurship? Are we starting from scratch? This understanding can help you set realistic expectations for progress toward energizing entrepreneurs.

You can also use the scores for individual readiness factors to identify those parts of the community's environment that may require special attention as you develop an entrepreneurship strategy. If your score on *Openness to Entrepreneurship* is low, you might want to ramp up your public relations efforts quickly to begin introducing the community to its successful entrepreneurs in very visible ways—a celebrate "homegrown" entrepreneurs day or ribbon cutting. If your *Beyond Town Borders* score is low, you might want to charge a committee of town leaders with the immediate task of identifying and connecting with regional service providers who might bring additional resources to your local entrepreneurs.

**TOOLS FOR
READINESS
ASSESSMENT**

TOOL 2
(continued)

**TOOLS FOR
READINESS
ASSESSMENT**

TOOL 3

Tool 3 – Rural Community Entrepreneurship Survey

When using this interview tool, it is important to assure the respondent that all information will remain confidential. You will want to express this in your own words. Below is an example of how you might introduce the survey to the person you are interviewing.

"The purpose of this survey is to gain a better understanding of how our community supports entrepreneurs, from the entrepreneurs' perspective. Your responses will be kept completely confidential and none of your individual information will be disclosed. We appreciate your willingness to share your story with us! Contact information will be used only if follow-up questions are necessary and to provide general demographic information for all those completing the survey."

Rural Community Entrepreneurship Survey

Name of owner _____

Address _____

City _____ State _____ Zip _____

Phone _____ Fax _____

Email _____

Website (if applicable) _____

Gender [ ] Male [ ] Female

Marital status: [ ] Single [ ] Married [ ] Separated [ ] Divorced

Number of children _____

Highest level of education completed
[ ] Eighth grade   [ ] High school   [ ] Trade school
[ ] College   [ ] Grad school

How many total years of personal business experience do you have?

_____

Was either of your parents ever involved in owning and operating their own business? [ ] Yes [ ] No

If yes, identify which parent and briefly describe the business activity.

_____

_____

Please use this scale with the following statements and circle the best response.
1 *strongly disagree* 2 *disagree* 3 *not sure* 4 *agree* 5 *strongly agree*

Community Attitudes:

- Most people in my community understand that entrepreneurs
are critically important to the future of our community.   1 2 3 4 5
- Most people in my community really support entrepreneurs
when they fail and are trying again with a new business.   1 2 3 4 5
- Most people in my community really support someone
who is creating a new or expanding an existing business.   1 2 3 4 5
- Most people in my community would encourage a younger
person to pursue a career creating and growing a business.   1 2 3 4 5
- Most people in my community would like to create and
grow a business.   1 2 3 4 5

Entrepreneurial Support:

- My community recognizes and celebrates people who
create and grow local businesses.   1 2 3 4 5
- My community has developed programs to encourage
and support entrepreneurs to develop and grow.   1 2 3 4 5
- My community has a micro-lending program.   1 2 3 4 5
- My community offers business or entrepreneurial training.   1 2 3 4 5
- My community creates networking and mentoring
opportunities for entrepreneurs and local business persons.   1 2 3 4 5
- My community has access to venture capital and/or
angel investors.   1 2 3 4 5

Economic Development:

- My community has an economic development program.   1 2 3 4 5
- Good business ideas in my community can attract the
necessary financial capital to get them going.   1 2 3 4 5
- There are many people in my community who actively
support economic development efforts.   1 2 3 4 5
- The focus of my community's economic development efforts includes:
  - Business attraction   1 2 3 4 5
  - Supporting existing businesses   1 2 3 4 5
  - Working with only businesses in town   1 2 3 4 5
  - Working with both town and country businesses   1 2 3 4 5
  - Considering farms and ranches as part
of the business community   1 2 3 4 5
  - Helping new businesses get started   1 2 3 4 5
  - Other (specify):   1 2 3 4 5

**TOOLS FOR
READINESS
ASSESSMENT**

TOOL 3
(continued)

75

**TOOLS FOR
READINESS
ASSESSMENT**

TOOL 3
(continued)

Using Tool 3 to Assess Readiness

The *Rural Community Entrepreneurship Survey* was designed to gather information from entrepreneurs at the community level. The survey can be administered in a one-on-one interview or in a larger group of entrepreneurs. This survey can provide useful baseline data about a community's support for entrepreneurs. The data can be used to identify areas where support for entrepreneurs may be lacking, such as in the availability of financial capital. In addition, this survey can be used before and after a community investment in support of entrepreneurship to assess how entrepreneurs' attitudes toward the community may have changed. For example, if your community is creating a network for entrepreneurs, this survey could be used to collect data both before and after the creation of the network. The survey can also be adapted for use with community leaders. The questions under *Community Attitudes*, *Entrepreneurial Support*, and *Economic Development* could be posed to elected officials, economic development professionals, leaders of nonprofit organizations, and citizens in the community to gain a different perspective on the community environment in support of entrepreneurship.

After the Assessment — Targeting Readiness Factors

A lot of new knowledge about a community's readiness for an entrepreneurship development program has just come your way, and we have provided several tools for you to use in further assessing your community's readiness. What happens next?

Through any means possible, avoid inaction. The three readiness assessment tools have given you lots of specific information regarding your community. Share what you've learned broadly throughout your community. Now's the time to write that newspaper article or develop a brief presentation to share with civic groups throughout the community. This information can be used to generate enthusiasm for entrepreneurship development beyond the committed group of community leaders that initiated the readiness assessment process.

You have also identified strengths and challenges. Perhaps begin by focusing on the strengths and maximizing them. Celebrate your strengths as a way of generating some positive movement for entrepreneurship development. If youth entrepreneurship is a strength in your community, figure out a way for these young entrepreneurs to be celebrated at your next chamber meeting. And, taking it one step further, develop a mentoring network to link experienced entrepreneurs with these young people.

Most importantly, don't let a low readiness score derail your efforts. Remember the story of Ord, Nebraska. Look for potential partners in your state or region who can help you build capacity for entrepreneurship development in your community.

Additional Resources

We have developed cutting edge and comprehensive information to help your community or region determine your level of readiness for moving to an entrepreneurial economy. This resource includes background information about the key elements essential to readiness. There are also tools and protocols you can use to help your corner of rural America get ready for an entrepreneurial future. Go to the companion E^2 *Energizing Entrepreneurs* website at www.energizingentrepreneurs.org. Once there, click on "Readiness" to find resources that support the information in this chapter.

For further analysis on community infrastructure read two articles by Cornelia Butler Flora:

"Enhancing Community Capitals: The Optimization Equation." *Rural Development News* 21 (1): 1-2. www.ag.iastate.edu/centers/rdev/newsletter/mar97/enhance.comm.cap.html

"Building Social Capital: The Importance of Entrepreneurial Social Infrastructure." Rural Development News 21 (2): 1-2. www.ag.iastate.edu/centers/rdev/newsletter/june97/build-soc-capital.html

Clues to Rural Community Survival, by Vicki Luther and Milan Wall of the Heartland Center for Leadership Development, provides case studies of 18 thriving rural communities, with insights on why they are succeeding. www.heartlandcenter.info/publications.htm

For great research on the factors that influence successful community building and a good basic foundation for looking at community readiness check out *Community Building: What makes it Work?* by Paul Mattesich and Barbara Monsey. Second printing 2001. Published by the Amherst H. Wilder Foundation. www.wilder.org

The Organization of Hope: A Workbook for Rural Asset-Based Community Development. Luther Snow. The ABCD Institute and the Blandin Foundation. 2001. Evanston, Ill. Based on the work of John McKnight in asset-mapping, this offers another look at rural community development based on strengths, not deficits.

CHAPTER 7
ASSESSMENT

Building an Entrepreneurial Development System

When you have determined that your community is ready for entrepreneurship development, you need to turn your attention to building an Entrepreneurial Development System (EDS). In this chapter, we explore the nuts and bolts of assessment in building such a system. But first, let's focus a bit more on this concept of an EDS. The idea of an EDS is relatively, but not entirely, new. A quick scan of cutting-edge recent work illustrates some examples:

- In our early work with the Rural Entrepreneurship Initiative in Minnesota, the idea of entrepreneurial support organizations (ESOs) emerged. ESOs were communities, regions or areas served by development organizations that provided comprehensive support for entrepreneurs.
- Erik Pages, President and CEO of EntreWorks Consulting, employs the concept of an entrepreneurial environment. He talks about creating an environment in which entrepreneurs can thrive, just as living organisms do in the natural world. When the environment is robust and healthy, it can support more life. He argues the same is true with communities, regions and nations, and the entrepreneurs they support.
- Patrick Von Bargen, CEO of the Center for Venture Education, employs the concept of entrepreneurial ecolo-

gy, similar to that advocated by Erik Pages. He considers factors that can create a thriving ecology with high rates of entrepreneurship. As with ecology, there are keystone species. In entrepreneurial ecology, the keystone species is the *high growth entrepreneur.*

- Tom Lyons and Gregg Lichtenstein have offered another view employing a baseball farm system analogy. Their Entrepreneurial League System® (ELS) embraces this idea of a comprehensive, on-going system of support targeting entrepreneurs with different skill levels.

- Finally, Brian Dabson, Associate Director of the Rural Policy Research Institute and Co-Director of the RUPRI Center for Rural Entrepreneurship, in the landmark study by CFED for the W.K. Kellogg Foundation, *Mapping Rural Entrepreneurship,* employs the term entrepreneurial development system (EDS). An EDS is a comprehensive system of support for entrepreneurs with five key components:
  - Entrepreneurship education
  - Training and technical assistance for entrepreneurs
  - Capital access for entrepreneurs
  - Entrepreneurial networks
  - Entrepreneurial culture

Best practice about entrepreneurship around the world generally embraces a system of support approach. These systems are structured so that support focuses on the entrepreneurs or entrepreneurial team first and the business second. There is recognition that this is largely a human development strategy as much as it is an economic development strategy. Like public education in the United States, where educational access leads to an inherently stronger society and economy, the EDS invests in entrepreneurs who in turn build stronger communities and economies.

Successful entrepreneurial development practice generally embraces an asset-based development approach. We have touched on asset-based development in other parts of this book. Simply restated, asset-based development focuses on those assets that a community already has to create an entrepreneurial economy and society and builds from this starting point.

Our ultimate goal is to build an entrepreneurial development system that can encourage, nurture and support entrepreneurs.

Given that the most strategic and effective way to build an EDS over time is through asset-based development, then assessment becomes critically important.

Why Assessment?

Knowledge is the foundation for effective action. The process of assessment enables a community to collectively discover itself and create the opportunity for action. The assessment process must be specific and clearly linked to building better entrepreneurial development strategies. This process must be (1) on-going and (2) quick paced.

Assessment is fundamental to fully understanding the assets present in our communities for energizing economies and societies through entrepreneurship. Most community planning processes focus on *things*, such as schools, streets and taxes. Most economic development planning processes focus on sectors, businesses and jobs. This information is important, but it does not give a community all that is needed to build a strong entrepreneurship strategy.

An entrepreneurship assessment needs to provide insight on four basic assets. To begin, we need a good understanding of our community and its economy. Most traditional community and economic development studies can provide this information. Insight on demographics, economic structure, businesses, income, jobs and trends are all helpful. Chances are this part of the assessment process has already been done, and much of this information is sitting on a shelf at the chamber of commerce, development corporation, county or city offices.

Next, we need to clarify what the collective expectations for community economic development are, at the stakeholder and community levels. It is vitally important to clarify what kind of community we envision and know what kinds of development outcomes are broadly supported within the community. Again, chances are much of this work is already done, but it may be necessary to dust it off and review it. Building a development strategy without a community vision is a formula for disaster.

Entrepreneurs are the key to an entrepreneurial development

strategy. Therefore, the next assessment process focuses on the entrepreneurial talent present in the community. At this point, we are looking for people with the passion and desire to build better businesses and community institutions. Later in this chapter we will explore a step-by-step process for identifying, visiting and targeting entrepreneurial talent.

Finally, we need to take stock of development assets and build on traditional work in this area. Infrastructure, such as workforce, capital, buildings and water rates, are the foundation. A weak development infrastructure makes this work a lot harder. However, we want to explore the kinds of development assets that are particularly important to entrepreneurs and their creative development process. The presence of business services, mentors, resource networks, training programs and access to capital are very important.

Clarifying our development goals in light of our community's entrepreneurial talent and entrepreneurial development assets gives us the building blocks for highly strategic and effective system development. Understanding the reasoning behind assessment is important, because many rural communities and regions are often reluctant to do additional surveys, studies and assessments. By doing sound assessment, however, we can build a strategic game plan that is more likely to achieve desired economic and social development results.

Earlier in this chapter we provided an overview of entrepreneurial development systems or EDSs. Next we want to explore in more depth the elements of entrepreneurial environment with a strong rural community grounding. This information is based on our extensive travels throughout rural America since 1999 and the resulting insights about real communities supporting their local entrepreneurs.

Elements of an Entrepreneurial Environment

The concept of an entrepreneurial environment is one that most rural residents can relate to. It provides a ready way to understand assets, identify where the gaps are and set priorities for capacity building. As you review this information, start reflecting on where your community is exceptionally strong and where you think additional work needs to be done.

Steve Buttress, former head of state economic development agencies for Nebraska and Florida, offers one of our favorite definitions of economic development:

"Economic development is a choice.
It is willed within an economy.
Economic development occurs when local leaders
choose to identify, invest in, and develop
their comparative advantages to enable
workers, firms, farms, and industries
to better compete."

This definition implies a very intentional approach to economic development on the part of community leaders. Each generation of community leaders chooses (or does not choose) to enact development strategies that they hope will create economic opportunities for the community and its residents. They choose to create an environment in which entrepreneurs can flourish.

Ideally, entrepreneurs live and work within a circle of support that encourages and assists in the creative process of venture development. Within this circle of support is a community environment that at a minimum recognizes and values the role of entrepreneurs (both private and public) in developing the community. Optimally, this environment includes specific initiatives or activities. Three elements constitute a community's entrepreneurial environment: climate, infrastructure and support.

Community Climate

Local communities have little to say about macro economic issues such as trade, fiscal or monetary policies. The cost of money or regulations governing the export of food products is the purview of national governments. However, communities do play a fundamental role in creating a supportive and stimulating climate for entrepreneurship. A strong entrepreneurial climate can be characterized as follows:

AWARENESS of the potential role that entrepreneurs, particularly growth entrepreneurs, play in economic development.

RECOGNITION that entrepreneurs face many challenges including the likelihood of failure in one or more ventures. Communities must understand the essence of entrepreneurship and its dynamic nature of creation, growth and sometimes failure. Fair weather support for entrepreneurs will not create an enduring supportive entrepreneurial environment.

CULTURE that is accepting of the challenges that entrepreneurial failure and success can bring to social order. Rural culture can play a critically important role in supporting or limiting entrepreneurial behavior. In rural communities, a business failure may well mean that your neighbor does not get paid and your daughter is not invited to a birthday party. On the other hand, too much success may mean that your family becomes socially marginalized from the mainstream community. Rural communities by their very size are intimate and demand that residents contribute to social harmony. Too much failure, as well as too much success, can unbalance a rural community, creating strife and conflict.

ANONYMITY so that entrepreneurs have the space they need to succeed. To a traditional and socially ordered rural community, the behavior of an entrepreneur may seem odd or unacceptable. Rural communities, because of their small size and close personal nature, often cannot offer entrepreneurs the space and anonymity they need to be creative. While this may be difficult for the coffee shop crowd, it is one more element in creating a strong entrepreneurial environment.

QUALITY OF LIFE amenities are essential to meeting the private needs of entrepreneurs, their families, and workers. Entrepreneurs generally have families and, like everyone else in the community, they want good schools, churches, recreational facilities and entertainment amenities. Rural communities that are able to strike a good balance between local tax rates and high quality public services are best able to retain and recruit entrepreneurs. The low-cost community may have had the competitive advantage during the recruitment wars of the past generation, but entrepreneurship support requires a different decision-making calculus.

Community Infrastructure

Rural communities are often situated in high cost and low density markets or markets where access to diverse, high quality and affordable infrastructure is harder to develop and sustain. Government programs have worked to ensure universal infrastructure ranging from banking services to telecommunications. However, in the era of deregulation, rural America is increasingly challenged to keep pace with state of the art infrastructure.

REAL ESTATE Entrepreneurs need different kinds of space in which to operate during different stages of development. In the early stages, an entrepreneur may need to set up the enterprise in a spare room in the home or a garage. Eventually, as the entrepreneurial enterprise grows, different kinds of space ranging from downtown storefronts to industrial park space will be needed. Availability of a range of real estate, or the ability to meet these needs as the entrepreneur grows the firm, is a critical element in building a supportive entrepreneurial environment.

UTILITIES Water, power and telecommunications are fundamental utilities central to the needs of commerce. Like any business, entrepreneurial businesses require sound and affordable utilities to be competitive. Rural communities often operate or regulate these utilities and therefore have influence over their offering and cost.

SERVICES Access to general business services such as banking, insurance, freight and accounting are as important to entrepreneurs as to any business. Massive consolidation of such services has changed and often reduced access to these basic services. Rural communities that are committed to ensuring local access to basic business services will create a more competitive entrepreneurial environment.

TAXES AND REGULATIONS No matter where entrepreneurs operate, they will face a wide range of local taxes and regulations. The nature and rates of taxation and regulation can be a barrier to entrepreneurial development, particularly in the start-up phase of an enterprise. However, often the size of the tax or complying with a certain regulation is not as big a challenge as the administration of these policies. Clear information on what a business must comply with and one-stop servicing can ease the burden of red tape and create a more supportive entrepreneurial environment.

Here's a final thought about infrastructure. To be equally competitive, rural communities must basically provide the same economic infrastructure that much larger and richer places provide. Successful communities pursue "real time" infrastructure development. Through their active communications with businesses and entrepreneurs, these communities have a good idea of what infrastructure investments are necessary to keep their entrepreneurs growing, and they act on those needs. This is one of the more powerful approaches to offset the size (or lack of size) challenge faced by most rural communities.

Community Support

A community can do a wide range of things to proactively support entrepreneurs. There is no single set of actions that a community should adopt. However, we find it useful to think about possible investments in three categories: basic, advanced and high performing levels of support.

BASIC SUPPORT Investment in a basic support package is the starting point to building a broader and more sophisticated community support system for entrepreneurs.

- A community should address any issues related to creating a positive *climate and strong infrastructure* for entrepreneurs. The greatest entrepreneurship development program operating in a weak climate with poor infrastructure will come up short.
- Before public programs are created, a community should take stock of its current access to appropriate *business services* (e.g., legal, marketing, production, financial, accounting). Access to the *right* services is important. Remember, having these services within the community is great, but not necessary to ensuring access.

- A community should create a *focus on entrepreneurs*, both public (those who build communities) and private (those who build businesses). Creating a focus on entrepreneurs might include raising the awareness level of community residents and leaders about the role of entrepreneurship within the community. Going a bit further, a community might identify entrepreneurs and provide periodic recognition for their contributions to the community. Most importantly, a community should value entrepreneurs and their unique role in building the community and the economy.
- Entrepreneurs themselves indicate that the most important support they can receive is *networking* with other entrepreneurs and access to *mentors*. Communities can create regular opportunities that encourage networking and mentoring.

ADVANCED SUPPORT Once the basic elements of a support system are in place, a community can consider a number of advanced activities to further energize entrepreneurs. Remember, more advanced support doesn't mean that things should become more complicated for the entrepreneur. Massive directories and complicated pathways for entrepreneurs to access support can be counterproductive. We urge communities at this level to create some kind of simple organization (probably using existing organizations) to ensure that entrepreneurial support efforts are understandable, easy to access and seamless.

- A community might want to offer an entrepreneurial training resource such as FastTrac, NxLeveL, or REAL (Rural Entrepreneurship through Action Learning). These programs are particularly helpful to start-up and early stage businesses.
- A community may want to ensure that an entrepreneur has access to appropriate financial capital beyond that provided by local banking institutions. The development of micro lending services for smaller start-up entrepreneurs and revolving loan programs for growing and restructuring businesses are likely first steps in building a stronger financial capital system for entrepreneurs.
- A community may want to implement programs that increase local entrepreneurs' awareness of and access to

new markets. In rural areas particularly, entrepreneurs may need assistance to develop strong skills in identifying market opportunities and assessing the commercial feasibility of various opportunities. Sending delegations to conferences, trade shows and trade missions are all good ways to increase market awareness.

- Communities should consider programming that introduces youth (the younger the better, starting in kindergarten) to entrepreneurship. Young people are a driving cultural force in our nation and communities. Sooner or later, these same young people will form the backbone of our economies and communities. Creating opportunities for young people to engage in venture and community building is critically important.

HIGH PERFORMING SUPPORT To be a high performing community that is optimally supporting entrepreneurs requires considerable community commitment and investment.

- Communities should consider strategies that offer customized help to the full range of local entrepreneurs. It requires a major community commitment to hire skilled entrepreneurial facilitators or coaches who work one on one with entrepreneurs.
- Sooner or later, growing ventures need more sophisticated forms of capital, including access to equity capital. Communities should consider building on current financing resources by creating area-based angel investment networks and pathways to more traditional venture capital resources (generally external to the community). As entrepreneurial deals emerge and grow, the ability to help these ventures meet their capital needs is key to keeping these businesses within the community.
- High performing communities find ways to integrate entrepreneurial opportunities into the core curriculum of their K-16 educational systems. Trying to engage youth in entrepreneurship via extracurricular activities is a real challenge and promises only marginal support. Quality time for entrepreneurship is a critical next step in building an entrepreneurial culture.
- Places with higher levels of entrepreneurial activity are

often places with high capacity organizations dedicated to supporting entrepreneurs. These entrepreneurial support organizations (ESOs) are rooted in communities and provide a more comprehensive and sophisticated package of support that energizes start-up entrepreneurs and grows entrepreneurial growth companies.

Relatively few communities in rural America meet the standards for a *high performing support environment*. Places like Fairfield, Iowa; Littleton, Colorado; and Douglas, Georgia, come close. Many more rural communities are providing *advanced support* to their entrepreneurs and even more have in place the basic elements of support. We hope you can use this information to gain some insight into where your region or community might be. However, you will likely need to engage in assessment to gain a deeper understanding, highlight your assets and craft the optimal game plan. In the next section, we explore a four-part assessment process that can help you do exactly that.

A Four-Part Assessment Process

As described earlier in this chapter, the four-part assessment process includes the following activities:

- **Developing your baseline**
- **Articulating your development vision and goals**
- **Mapping and targeting your entrepreneurial talent**
- **Identifying your entrepreneurial development assets**

Let's explore each part of this process in detail.

Part I. Developing Your Baseline

The baseline assessment is an important first step. In many ways, it provides the overall context for building a community entrepreneurship strategy that makes the best sense. Most of the time, this is review work. Many communities have multiple economic and demographic studies already on the shelf. Local universities and state/regional development agencies have much of this information. As a first step, we urge you to review these reports and pull out information that would be helpful to building an entrepreneurship strategy.

RESOURCES TO GUIDE YOUR ASSESSMENT PROCESS

As you undertake this assessment process, you may be looking for more resources to guide you. Through our companion website, www.energizingentrepreneurs.org, you can get more information to help you complete all four parts of this assessment process.

The baseline assessment should include an understanding of these community elements:

- The community's socio-economic profile, including some history of culture and tradition, particularly related to entrepreneurship; the structure of the local economy, including your Main Street businesses; any community-specific information such as large numbers of Main Street entrepreneurs near retirement or the impending construction of a regional health care facility.
- Leadership and civic capacity, including an understanding of who are the champions for entrepreneurship and the capacity of local development organizations.
- Development capacity, an initial scan of economic development goals and where entrepreneurship fits, along with any specific tools or capacities for entrepreneurship development that exist in your community.
- Entrepreneurial talent, initial insights from knowledgeable leaders about the entrepreneurs in your community.

While much of this baseline assessment will be review, it's important to look at past studies with a new eye focused on entrepreneurship. Identify those aspects of your community's economy that create particular opportunities for or challenges to entrepreneurs. You may want to put together some summary observations and share them with others in your community. Making a brief presentation to the chamber or to local government officials can help you gain additional insights about your local community that will contribute to developing your baseline.

Part II.
Articulating Development Vision and Goals

Clarifying a community's development vision and goals is an important step in this process. We suggest two key activities. First, have your working team review existing community studies and surveys where vision and goal information has already been compiled. Pull out those items that relate to building an entrepreneurial community. This information ensures that you build from earlier work. However, it is also important to give your community a chance to gain current insight.

On Page 95 you will find a tool, Identifying Community Economic Development Outcomes, to help you identify what your community hopes to achieve, consistent with the vision and goals you've established. Start by summarizing the vision and goals information from previous studies. Remember, we're building on all the good work your community has done already! Then you can use this survey in several ways.

Start with your leadership team and explore their attitudes, desires and thinking about development needs and goals. Then, engage your stakeholder groups—the folks you want on your team, and cannot afford to have off the team! These might include the local chamber executive, economic developer, local government officials, or editor of the local paper, among others. Finally, create some opportunities for broader community awareness building and engagement. You might consider conducting forums at civic club meetings, doing stories through your local media that include the survey or creating display boards for public places with surveys attached.

At this point, we have completed two important assessments. We have organized existing community and economic information to provide the context for strategy building. We have also revised our community's vision and development expectations. We are now ready to undertake the third assessment—discovering entrepreneurial talent.

Part III.
Mapping and Targeting Entrepreneurial Talent

Entrepreneurship is an American value, rooted in our culture. We see ourselves as entrepreneurial in our passion to create and our motivation to build. Everyone who is in business probably has some entrepreneurial traits. But most business people are not entrepreneurs. True entrepreneurs represent a relatively small segment of American society. Entrepreneurs are those who have a passion for creating and a capacity for growing enterprises. Entrepreneurial talent is rooted in motivation and capacity. Both are learned traits and can be developed, expanding the nucleus of entrepreneurs at the community level.

Every community has a range of entrepreneurial talent. This part of the assessment helps economic development practitioners and community leaders better understand the local pool of entrepreneurial talent. One way to assess the types of entrepreneurial talent present in your community or region is through the use of talent mapping. A group of informed citizens can begin to identify specific entrepreneurs based on the typology presented here. Once you've mapped your entrepreneurs, you can begin to target specific entrepreneurs (for example, aspiring or growth-oriented) for visitation. Visitation, employing a business retention and expansion model, can provide deeper insight with respect to entrepreneurship traits and enterprise needs.

There are five steps to MAPPING AND TARGETING ENTREPRENEURIAL TALENT:

STEP 1 – BUILD A TEAM Pull together a team of folks who have considerable familiarity with the community, its residents and businesses. This team will provide the expertise for the entrepreneurial talent mapping work. Possible team members might include someone from the newspaper, local government, chamber of commerce, development corporation or bank.

STEP 2 – GATHER INFORMATIONAL RESOURCES Before the team meets to begin the mapping work, gather various information resources that might help identify possible entrepreneurial talent. These resources might include the local business directory, telephone book or other directories of local business people.

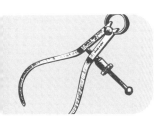

STEP 3 – IDENTIFY ENTREPRENEURIAL TALENT Once the team is gathered, **we have provided a tool, Identifying Entrepreneurial Talent, beginning on page 96** to identify and categorize businesses within the main entrepreneurial talent categories. Use the **Entrepreneurial Talent Checklist** as a guide to classify local entrepreneurs on the worksheet that follows. Remember, an entrepreneur doesn't need to meet all the items on a specific checklist to fall into that category. Use these characteristics as a guide in placing entrepreneurs. Use the **Entrepreneurial Talent Mapping Worksheet on page 98** to list as many entrepreneurs in each category as you can identify in your community. This is a first cut so don't worry about exact placement. This list will be used for further targeting.

STEP 4 – FOCUS, FOCUS, FOCUS Few communities or organizations have the capacity initially to work with all types of entrepreneurial talent. Focusing on those entrepreneurial talent groups that best fit your community's economic development

needs and support capacities is important. **Use the two-part tool, Targeting Entrepreneurial Talent, found on page 99** to help with this targeting activity. Start by working through the **Entrepreneurial Talent Pros and Cons Checklist (pages 99-100)** to get a better understanding of some of the benefits and challenges of targeting different types of entrepreneurial talent. Then, use the **Entrepreneurial Talent Pros and Cons Worksheet (page 101)** to create your own list of pros and cons for targeting each type of talent in your community or region.

STEP 5 – VISITATION Once your group has focused on the type of entrepreneurial talent that you will work with, plan visits to each and every entrepreneur on your list. The RUPRI Center for Rural Entrepreneurship has developed interview and survey tools that can guide you.

By working through these steps, you should have a good idea of who the entrepreneurs in your community are and what type of entrepreneurs your community should target initially as part of an entrepreneurship development strategy.

Part IV.
Identifying Entrepreneurial Development Assets

Energizing local entrepreneurial talent requires a supportive environment that can meet the needs of entrepreneurs on a real time basis. The Entrepreneurship Asset Mapping Process is intended to help a community identify and mobilize elements of a supportive system and environment.

THREE-STEP PROCESS

A three-step process is recommended that moves the community from discovery of what it has (as well as where the gaps are) to the beginning stages of building a system of support.

STEP 1 – SCANNING EXERCISE The first step in this process is the scanning exercise. A facilitated focus group is recommended as the best way to get this step completed. You should recruit three to seven individuals with good knowledge of development resources available to the community. You can use the team you put together to map your entrepreneurial talent, but you should also consider including members from outside the community who may help you complete this step more effective-

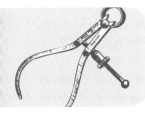

ly. The group should meet for 90 minutes to three hours (depending upon the size of the community). The **Entrepreneurship Asset Mapping Tool provided on pages 102 through 105** should be used to guide the scanning work.

We recommend that you start with the **Entrepreneurial Assets Checklist (page 102)** and check off all the programs and resources available in your community and region. Then complete a worksheet for each of the main categories in the checklist. Start with "programs" and proceed to "business services," and then "capital." (Remember, you've already identified your entrepreneurial talent in Part III above.) Try to be specific and identify known resources that fit into the categories within the checklist. Ultimately, these identified resources can be organized into a resource directory that the community can use to trigger assistance for entrepreneurs once needs and opportunities are identified.

STEP 2 – DOCUMENTATION Step two involves documenting that the assets identified during the scanning process really exist. It can also involve verifying the quality and capability of each resource. For example, the community may have sound attorneys, but their scope of service might not include specialized law such as intellectual property rights. The documentation process can best be undertaken as entrepreneurs are identified and visited, and as assistance programs are launched. This approach allows the community to focus on finding resources necessary to meet the immediate needs of its targeted entrepreneurs.

STEP 3 – SYSTEM BUILDING Ultimately, entrepreneurs need and want a system of support. They do not want a directory or an alphabet soup of supposed resources. What they need and want are safe (confidential) pathways to those resources that can help them with today's pressing challenges and opportunities. From the community's point of view, knowing what resources exist to help your entrepreneurs puts you in a stronger position to be responsive to the needs of entrepreneurs as they emerge.

ENTREPRENEURS AS ASSETS

The entrepreneurs in your communities are possibly the most powerful resource you have for energizing entrepreneurship. As you mapped your entrepreneurial talent, you probably have identified successful entrepreneurs with a rich range of experiences and knowledge. Now it's time to recognize these entrepreneurs as assets in your community. Networking, mentoring and peer opportunities can put these assets to use by connecting experienced entrepreneurs with those earlier in this process of creating and growing ventures.

Part II: Articulating Development Vision and Goals

Identifying Community Economic Development Outcomes

The following exercise is brief. Earlier visions and goals can be summarized on an information sheet and then this survey can be used to gain current and additional insight.

NEXT FIVE YEARS By the end of five years, identify the three to five economic development outcomes that you would consider desirable and achievable:

#	Desired Outcome
1	
2	
3	
4	
5	

THIS YEAR Over the coming year, identify three to five economic development outcomes that you would consider desirable and achievable:

#	Desired Outcome
1	
2	
3	
4	
5	

FOUR-PART ASSESSMENT PROCESS TOOLS AND WORKSHEETS

PART II: ARTICULATING DEVELOPMENT VISION AND GOALS

**FOUR-PART
ASSESSMENT
PROCESS
TOOLS AND
WORKSHEETS**

PART III:
MAPPING AND
TARGETING
ENTREPRENEURIAL
TALENT
STEP 3

Part III:
Mapping and Targeting Entrepreneurial Talent

Step 3 – Identifying Entrepreneurial Talent

This tool has two parts—first, the ENTREPRENEURIAL TALENT CHECKLIST provides descriptive characteristics for different types of entrepreneurial talent and should be used as a resource as you map your community's entrepreneurs. The second part—the ENTREPRENEURIAL TALENT MAPPING WORKSHEET provides space for you to identify and classify specific entrepreneurs in your community according to your understanding of their entrepreneurial talent. Remember, you may move entrepreneurs from one place on the worksheet to another as you visit with them and learn more about them.

Entrepreneurial Talent Checklist

POTENTIAL

Aspiring
[ ] Actively considering going into business
[ ] Actively researching a business idea
[ ] Attending business workshops
[ ] Networking and testing ideas with others
[ ] Motivated toward a life change

Start-ups
[ ] In the process of starting a business
[ ] May or may not have been in business before
[ ] May or may not have a good plan
[ ] Motivated to make this life change
[ ] May or may not have the necessary skills

BUSINESS OWNERS

Survival
[ ] Struggling to make enough income to sustain their families
[ ] Doing multiple things to generate enough income
[ ] Have difficulty seeing opportunities, such as new markets
[ ] Often stressed
[ ] Reluctant to seek out help

Lifestyle

[ ] Generally successful
[ ] Often well established
[ ] Not actively seeking to change business model
[ ] Not actively seeking to grow
[ ] Have established and comfortable goals

Re-Starts

[ ] Have been in business before with limited success
[ ] In the process of starting a new business
[ ] Recognize weaknesses in business skills
[ ] Motivated to succeed this time around
[ ] Willing to seek out help

ENTREPRENEURS

Growth-Oriented

[ ] Successful in business
[ ] Have a growth orientation and drive
[ ] Actively seeking new markets, services and products
[ ] Open to new ideas and seeking new insights
[ ] Seeking to be more competitive

Serial

[ ] History of creating and growing more than one business
[ ] Tend to move on to a new business idea quickly
[ ] Often sell a business start-up once it is up and running
[ ] Generally on the lookout for new ideas and opportunities
[ ] May have multiple business interests going at one time

Entrepreneurial Growth Companies

[ ] Experiencing rapid growth in employment or sales
[ ] Reaching new markets
[ ] Developing new products and services
[ ] Experiencing growth in customers or users
[ ] Innovative and dynamic leadership and workforce

FOUR-PART ASSESSMENT PROCESS TOOLS AND WORKSHEETS

PART III: MAPPING AND TARGETING ENTREPRENEURIAL TALENT STEP 3
(continued)

FOUR-PART ASSESSMENT PROCESS TOOLS AND WORKSHEETS

PART III: MAPPING AND TARGETING ENTREPRENEURIAL TALENT STEP 3

(continued)

Entrepreneurial Talent Mapping Worksheet

ASPIRING	RE-STARTS
START-UPS	GROWTH-ORIENTED
SURVIVAL	SERIAL
LIFESTYLE	ENTREPRENEURIAL GROWTH COMPANIES

Part III:
Mapping and Targeting Entrepreneurial Talent
Step 4 –
Focus, Focus, Focus

Use this two-part tool to help you target entrepreneurs within your community. Start by working through the ENTREPRENEURIAL TALENT PROS AND CONS CHECKLIST to get a better understanding of some of the benefits and challenges of targeting different types of entrepreneurial talent. Then, use the ENTREPRENEURIAL TALENT PROS AND CONS WORKSHEET to create your own list of pros and cons for targeting each type of talent in your community or region.

Entrepreneurial Talent Pros and Cons Checklist

Entrepreneurial Type	Pros of Targeting	Cons of Targeting
Potential - Youth	Large pool Can be change agents Can energize a community	Long-term commitment Create indirect outcomes Significant cost/outcomes
Potential - Aspiring	Large pool Primed to go Modest early impact Medium-term incubation	Long-term commitment Subsidized assistance Modest outcomes
Potential - Start-ups	Modest pool Commitment to go Assistance critical Modest impact	Subsidized assistance Medium-term incubation Modest outcomes

Business Owners - Survival	Already committed
	Some business experience
	Qualified motivation
	Tipping point opportunity
	  for community
	Large pool
		Challenged and struggling
		Bad habits and attitudes
		Wrong or incomplete
		  motivation
		Modest investment
		  required
		Long-term opportunity

Business Owners - Lifestyle	Already committed
	Some business experience
	Often successful
	Tipping point opportunity
	  for community
	Modest investment
		May lack motivation to
		  grow
		Modest pool

FOUR-PART
ASSESSMENT
PROCESS
TOOLS AND
WORKSHEETS

PART III:
MAPPING AND
TARGETING
ENTREPRENEURIAL
TALENT
STEP 4

FOUR-PART ASSESSMENT PROCESS TOOLS AND WORKSHEETS

PART III: MAPPING AND TARGETING ENTREPRENEURIAL TALENT STEP 4
(continued)

Entrepreneurial Type	Pros of Targeting	Cons of Targeting
Business Owners – Re-Starts	Strong business experience Motivated to succeed Opportunity for impact	History of failure Bad habits and attitudes Need to market test the opportunity
Entrepreneurs - Growth-oriented	Successful at business Motivated to grow Often open to help Opportunity for high impact Opportunity for immediate impact	Small pool Some are negative on help Weak self-awareness Requires time to build a relationship Limited ability to help
Entrepreneurs - Serial	High impact Remarkable assets Civic leadership and can become patrons	Very small pool Limited ability to help May lack patience and be demanding
Entrepreneurs - Entrepreneurial Growth Companies	Achieving growth Realizing impact Home run potential Civic leadership and can become patrons	Rare Negative or demanding on help Require higher order help Relocation threat

Entrepreneurial Talent Pros And Cons Worksheet

Entrepreneurial Type	Pros of Targeting	Cons of Targeting
Potential – Youth		
Potential – Aspiring		
Potential – Start-Ups		
Business Owners – Survival		
Business Owners – Lifestyle		
Business Owners – Re-Starts		
Entrepreneurs – Growth Oriented		
Entrepreneurs – Serial		
Entrepreneurs – Entrepreneurial Growth Companies		

FOUR-PART ASSESSMENT PROCESS TOOLS AND WORKSHEETS

PART III: MAPPING AND TARGETING ENTREPRENEURIAL TALENT STEP 4
(continued)

**FOUR-PART
ASSESSMENT
PROCESS
TOOLS AND
WORKSHEETS**

**PART IV:
IDENTIFYING
ENTREPRENEURIAL
ASSETS
STEP 1**

Part IV: Identifying Entrepreneurial Assets

Step 1 – Scanning Exercise

Starting with the Entrepreneurial Assets Checklist, check off all the programs and resources available in your community and region. Then complete a worksheet for each of the main categories in the checklist. Start with the Entrepreneurship Programs Worksheet, proceed to the Business Services Worksheet and then on to the Capital Programs Worksheet. (Remember, you've already identified your Entrepreneurs in Part III above.) Try to be specific and identify known resources that fit into the categories within the checklist.

Entrepreneurship Asset Mapping Tool

ENTREPRENEURIAL ASSETS CHECKLIST

Entrepreneurship Programs	**Business Services**
[ ] Mentors/Peer Groups	[ ] Accounting
[ ] Self-Awareness Assistance	[ ] Legal
[ ] Assessment	[ ] Human Resources
[ ] Training	[ ] Information Technology
[ ] Marketing	[ ] Financing
[ ] Business Plan Development	[ ] Business Transfer Planning
[ ] Feasibility Studies	[ ] Production
[ ] Technical Assistance	[ ] Marketing
[ ] Specialized Assistance	[ ] Market Identification & Development

Capital	**Entrepreneurs**
[ ] Literacy	[ ] Aspiring
[ ] Micro Lending	[ ] Start-ups
[ ] Revolving Loan Funds	[ ] Survival
[ ] Commercial Lenders	[ ] Life Style
[ ] State/Federal Program Linkages	[ ] Re-Start
[ ] Angel Investors	[ ] Growth Oriented
[ ] Seed Capital	[ ] Serial
[ ] Venture Capital	[ ] High Growth Company

Use the tools "Identifying Entrepreneurial Talent" on page 96 and "Targeting Entrepreneurial Talent" on page 99 to help you complete this part of the checklist.

Entrepreneurship Asset Mapping Tool

BUSINESS SERVICES WORKSHEET

ACCOUNTING	LEGAL
HUMAN RESOURCES	FINANCING
BUSINESS TRANSFER PLANNING	PRODUCTION CONSULTING
MARKETING & MARKET DEVELOPMENT	OTHER?

FOUR-PART ASSESSMENT PROCESS TOOLS AND WORKSHEETS

PART IV: IDENTIFYING ENTREPRENEURIAL ASSETS STEP 1 (continued)

Note: Not all business services are equal. Some services can address basic needs such as financial bookkeeping while others can handle the complicated issues of business transfer planning. One way to assess the capacity of the service is to look at the kinds of clients it serves. Clients with complicated and sizeable business structures indicate that the business service has higher capacity levels.

**FOUR-PART
ASSESSMENT
PROCESS
TOOLS AND
WORKSHEETS**

**PART IV:
IDENTIFYING
ENTREPRENEURIAL
ASSETS
STEP 1**
(continued)

Entrepreneurship Asset Mapping Tool

ENTREPRENEURSHIP PROGRAMS WORKSHEET

MENTOR/PEER GROUPS PROGRAMS	AWARENESS & ASSESSMENT PROGRAMS
MARKET DEVELOPMENT & MARKETING PROGRAMS	BUSINESS PLAN DEVELOPMENT & FEASIBILITY STUDY SUPPORT
TECHNICAL ASSISTANCE PROGRAMS (1)	TRAINING PROGRAMS (2)
SPECIALIZED ASSISTANCE PROGRAMS (3)	OTHER?

(1) *Examples of technical assistance programs might include manufacturing extension, cooperative extension, Small Business Development Centers, SCORE, and programs associated with incubator facilities.*

(2) *Examples of training programs might include FastTrac, NxLeveL, REAL, Core Four and other similar programs.*

(3) *Examples of specialized programs include the technology transfer and commercialization programs at universities, the Import/Export Bank, and e-commerce programs.*

Entrepreneurship Asset Mapping Tool

CAPITAL PROGRAMS WORKSHEET

FINANCIAL LITERACY (1)	MICRO LENDING PROGRAMS
REVOLVING LOAN PROGRAMS	COMMERCIAL LENDERS
LINKAGES TO STATE & FEDERAL FINANCING PROGRAMS	LOCAL ANGEL INVESTORS
SEED, VENTURE & EQUITY INVESTORS	OTHER?

FOUR-PART ASSESSMENT PROCESS TOOLS AND WORKSHEETS

PART IV: IDENTIFYING ENTREPRENEURIAL ASSETS STEP 1 (continued)

(1) *Financial literacy relates to the entrepreneur's knowledge and experience with various forms of capital and financing arrangements. Strategies to help entrepreneurs become more capital aware are critically important.*

Note: Chances are that multiple capital resources exist. Whether private or public, these resources are often complicated to use and challenge the entrepreneur. Creating help within the community to assist the entrepreneur work through the red tape of these programs is important to building a capital rich environment.

Additional Resources

You'll find a number of helpful resources for assessment on our companion website for this book at www.energizingentrepreneurs.org. Click on "Assessment" to locate and download the tools and worksheets we have included at the end of this chapter.

You will find a number of tools that practitioners have found useful in their communities. As you move forward with your assessment activities, you might want to look at some of the materials produced in other communities. On our website, you will find a generic baseline assessment completed by a rural community like yours. This assessment report will give you a better idea of the type of information you might want to pull together for your community.

The final step in completing the Mapping and Targeting Entrepreneurial Talent assessment is to visit entrepreneurs in your community. To help guide this visitation process, we have developed a number of tools or visitation protocols. In addition to the generic Entrepreneur Visitation Protocol that you can find on our website, there are tools for you to use with entrepreneurs engaged in different types of businesses:

- **Tourism Related Visitation Protocol**
- **Transfer Business Visitation Protocol**
- **Growth Business Visitation Protocol**

We invite you to use and adapt these tools with the entrepreneurs you visit in your communities.

CHAPTER 8
STRATEGIES FOR
ENERGIZING
ENTREPRENEURS

Understanding Entrepreneurial Talent in Practice

Building on the assessment process you've completed, it is time to create an entrepreneurship development strategy for your community. Few communities, if any, have the resources and capacity to build a strategy that effectively serves all types of entrepreneurs. Your assessment helped you figure out who your entrepreneurs are and what types of entrepreneurs you should target in the initial stages of an entrepreneurship development system. Now we describe how you can tailor your development strategy to the types of entrepreneurs you are targeting. Let's start by reviewing the concept of entrepreneurial talent.

In Chapter 4, we described the following types of entrepreneurial talent:

- **Type 1 – Limited Potential**
- **Type 2 – Potential Entrepreneurs**
- **Type 3 – Business Owners**
- **Type 4 – Entrepreneurs**
- **Type 5 – Civic Entrepreneurs**

Now we want to focus on entrepreneurial talent in practice—the entrepreneurs present in your community who currently have (or could have) the potential to impact your local economy: *potential entrepreneurs, business owners and entrepreneurs.* (We'll talk more about limited potential and civic entrepreneurs later in

IN THIS CHAPTER

> **Understanding Entrepreneurial Talent in Practice**

> **Finding the Sweet Spot**

> **Targeting Strategies to Entrepreneurial Type**

> **Elements of Successful Practice**

the chapter.) As you make decisions about what types of entrepreneurs to target with your development strategy, it is important to understand how long it may take to achieve impact and what the scale of that impact might be for each type of entrepreneurial talent. Here are some insights for each type.

Potential Entrepreneurs

Potential entrepreneurs are those who have some of the skills and the motivation to embark on venture creation, but they may not have yet taken the plunge. Included here are aspiring and start-up entrepreneurs who are actively engaged in planning for or starting their own businesses, along with those who are experiencing some frustration with the process. Young people who are "kicking the tires" of entrepreneurship through school or after-school programs may also have the motivation and commitment that places them in this category. In addition, there are the dreamers—those who have the spark of entrepreneurship but need someone to fan the flames.

Your assessment should have helped you identify some of these potential entrepreneurs in your community and, chances are, there are plenty of them. However, it will likely take time, and lots of it, to help these potential entrepreneurs achieve their ultimate goal of starting their own business. How long might it take to move a local potter, dreaming in her studio, from the dream of a Main Street art gallery to the reality of a grand opening? The task of cultivating dreams and helping an entrepreneur develop the skills needed to be successful doesn't happen in weeks (or even months). Focusing on potential entrepreneurs is a long-term strategy, but one that will help to fill your community's pipeline with entrepreneurs for the future. You are unlikely to see immediate and measurable outcomes that will help you gain community support for your efforts.

What about the scale of impact? This could range from limited—a few ventures providing employment for the entrepreneurs alone—to quite large if the support system is successful in helping potential entrepreneurs develop the skills and capture the resources needed to create new businesses.

Business Owners

As you worked through your community assessment, you

may have had a conversation like this one:

Team Member #1: "What about Joe Sportingoods? What type of entrepreneur is Joe?"

Team Member #2: "I'm not sure Joe really is an entrepreneur. He's been running his business the same way for years—just like his father did. Is that an entrepreneur?"

Most business owners are not entrepreneurs. They have found a comfortable way of doing business that works for them and they may have little need for or motivation to change. However, there are some business owners who may have strong entrepreneurial tendencies. Think about business owners in your community who are trying out new business models. Joe Sportingoods may be testing ways to tap regional markets through the Internet. The local pharmacist may be in the midst of transferring the business to her daughter who has innovative ideas about how to create a new type of pharmacy and reach new markets for compounded pharmaceuticals.

The trick with business owners is to try to understand what their motivations are and where they want to take their businesses. Then it is possible to target those who are true entrepreneurs—working on their business every day to identify and take advantage of new opportunities to improve and grow their ventures. Once you've found these entrepreneurial business owners, the time to achieve some level of impact may be shorter than if you targeted potential entrepreneurs. These entrepreneurs are already in business and have a set of resources and skills that the potential entrepreneurs may lack. The scale of impact may be modest, if these business owners improve but don't grow their ventures—but it could be large for those who are actively interested in growing their businesses.

Entrepreneurs

The entrepreneurs in your community are those who are actively seeking new markets, developing new products or services, and exploring new ways of doing business. You will probably find far fewer entrepreneurs than you will business owners and most of those will be what we describe as "growth oriented." These entrepreneurs are seeking to grow their businesses and are looking for opportunities and support to do just that. You may also have found some "serial entrepreneurs"—those who start and

---

OPPORTUNITY VS. NECESSITY ENTREPRENEURS

Entrepreneurs may choose to create ventures because they see opportunities and are driven to exploit them. An entrepreneur in southeastern Kentucky created a business of adult day care facilities because the lack of quality care for elders in Appalachia was forcing children to leave their jobs to care for elderly parents, hurting everyone in the family. Other entrepreneurs create businesses out of necessity—self-

(continued on next page)

(Opportunity vs. Necessity continued)

employment or setting up a business becomes a way to stay in the region or make ends meet when times are tough. Laid off from a high-tech job, an entrepreneur turns to his love of blacksmithing to provide income and occupation, at least until the market for his high-tech skills gets strong again. Why do you need to understand the difference? A necessity entrepreneur may have no interest in growth (and therefore support services) while the opportunity entrepreneur may be actively seeking growth and need all the support you can provide.

grow a business and then sell that business and start another one. Serial entrepreneurs use their expertise to create ventures but then seek out new opportunities to begin the process anew rather than staying with one venture for the long haul.

Rare in most rural communities are the entrepreneurial growth companies. These are the rapidly growing businesses (also called gazelles) that we frequently associate with entrepreneurs such as Bill Gates, Steve Jobs and Sam Walton. If you find them in your community, you should cultivate them not only for the potential impact on your economy, but also for their ability to serve as mentors or role models for the other entrepreneurs you are supporting.

Entrepreneurs may be fewer in number in your community, but they can have a short-term (perhaps immediate) and large impact on your economy. A growth-oriented business may create wealth for the entrepreneur, as well as jobs and wealth for the employees of the growing venture.

Finding the Sweet Spot

In any economic development activity, it's important to aim for what we call the "sweet spot." This is where the goals for economic development correspond to the assets available for economic development in such a way that a strategic focus emerges. In entrepreneurship development, we are looking for that place where the types of entrepreneurs in your community overlap with your development assets placed within the context of your community's development goals. Sometimes a picture's worth a thousand words—the graphic here illustrates the "sweet spot" for entrepreneurship development.

As you move forward with strategy development, it's important to keep in mind this "sweet spot." For example, many rural communities in North Carolina and other southern states are searching for ways to help displaced textile mill work-

Finding the Sweet Spot

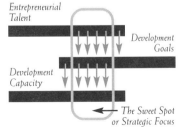

Entrepreneurial Talent

Development Goals

Development Capacity

The Sweet Spot or Strategic Focus

ers get back to work, often by making their own jobs through entrepreneurship. These displaced workers form a large pool of potential entrepreneurs, and helping those in this pool create new ventures is a key development goal in many of these communities. While it may take time, some communities are committed to working, one potential entrepreneur at a time, to achieve this goal. Their strategy is to use entrepreneurship education assets, specifically REAL "how to start a business" classes offered at no cost through community colleges, coupled with the availability of micro loans through the North Carolina Rural Economic Development Center, to provide opportunities to a new generation of entrepreneurs.

Targeting Strategies to Entrepreneurial Type

Just as the skills, motivations and characteristics vary by type of entrepreneurs in any community, the strategies for supporting entrepreneurs will also vary by type. You need to develop a strategy that effectively serves the specific types of entrepreneurs that you have decided to target as part of your overall entrepreneurship development strategy. To illustrate how to target strategies, let's focus on four specific types of entrepreneurs:

- **Aspiring and start-ups**
- **Youth**
- **Growth-oriented**
- **Entrepreneurial growth companies**

The real key is to understand what each type of entrepreneur needs and wants then implement strategies that give them that assistance and support.

Strategies for Aspiring and Start-Up Entrepreneurs

Aspiring and start-up entrepreneurs are early in the venture creation process. Aspiring entrepreneurs may still be researching and developing their business idea. They may even be testing it out in informal ways. Start-up entrepreneurs have made the decision to move forward and often have some plan for doing so. A common characteristic of both groups, however, is that they need help and support.

Aspiring entrepreneurs need guidance in assessing how good their idea really is. Will it meet a market test? Will someone pay for the good or service they want to offer? Is it really feasible for them to create this business? They need someone to ask the tough questions so that they can make an informed "go—no go" decision about starting a business.

Start-ups also need someone who can help them move from ideas to a solid game plan. They have already made a decision to start a business—now they need help making sure all the pieces are in place. Is the management team strong? Is there capital to start the venture? Are markets clearly identified and strategies for tapping them tested?

What strategies will meet the needs of these entrepreneurs? There are four basic approaches that are effective with these entrepreneurs:

- Networking and mentoring
- Microenterprise programs
- Entrepreneurship training and business counseling programs
- Facilitation and coaching

NETWORKING AND MENTORING   Entrepreneurial networks that serve aspiring and start-up entrepreneurs can be both formal and informal. Formal networks can have a wide range—from monthly forums sponsored by the chamber of commerce that offer an opportunity for entrepreneurs to meet their peers and share information about service providers, markets or frustrations about doing business—to the national model for an entrepreneurial network, the Council for Entrepreneurial Development.

However, networking doesn't have to be this formal. In one small community, an effective network was created with a front porch and willing participants. When an entrepreneur moved back to his hometown to start his business, he was looking for opportunities to meet other entrepreneurs in town. So he offered refreshments and his front porch (or his hearth during winter months) on Friday afternoons to entrepreneurs in the community who wanted to meet and talk about their businesses. This informal network became a place for sharing problems, identifying opportunities, testing out new ideas and providing support to one another—meeting a vital need in this small town.

For both start-ups and aspiring entrepreneurs, having an opportunity to talk with other entrepreneurs who have "been there, done that" is a valuable experience. While this may occur in a network, mentoring programs can be effective in strategically linking an experienced entrepreneur with an aspiring or start-up entrepreneur. Mentoring can happen organically. For example, experienced Hispanic restaurant owners in Hendersonville, North Carolina, "adopted" new immigrants who were interested in starting restaurants or catering businesses to help them learn the ins and outs of the sector. Mentoring programs can also be established by creating a pool of experienced entrepreneurs who are willing to work with new entrepreneurs in sectors where they have expertise.

Council for Entrepreneurial Development

"By entrepreneurs, for entrepreneurs" is the motto of the nationally recognized Council for Entrepreneurial Development (CED) in the Research Triangle region of North Carolina. Established in 1984, CED is a private, nonprofit organization whose mission is to "identify, enable and promote high growth, high impact companies and accelerate the entrepreneurial culture of the Research Triangle region." CED has 3,500 active members from over 1,000 companies, making it the largest entrepreneurial support organization in the country.

CED was founded by several business leaders in the region who wanted to create a network for entrepreneurs to share information and gain better access to services, including venture capital. Now, CED offers a wide range of programs to its entrepreneur members, including:

- FastTrac training programs
- Innovators Workshop
- Biotech, Infotech, Entrepreneur and Venture Conferences
- Biotech, Tech and BIO Investor Forums
- CFO Roundtable
- Entrepreneurial Excellence Awards

All of these programs grew out of a stated need on the part of

CED's members. Programs are designed with input from entrepreneurs and support from CED staff. The key metric used by the staff to determine the value of their programs is "was this the most valuable use of your time or would you have been better off spending the time working on your business?" This is an exacting standard, but it helps to keep CED focused on responding to and meeting the needs of entrepreneurs.

While CED's region is not rural, the model has been replicated in other more rural parts of the state including western North Carolina (Blue Ridge Entrepreneurial Council) and the central Piedmont region (Piedmont Triad Entrepreneurial Network). To learn more about CED, go to www.cednc.org.

MICROENTERPRISE PROGRAMS Microenterprise programs combine access to small amounts of capital with training in financial literacy and business development. Effective programs couple capital with training so that aspiring and start-up entrepreneurs have an opportunity to develop the business management skills needed to run a business at the same time as they get a loan to get the business off the ground. These programs are targeted to small entrepreneurs (less than five employees), usually the self-employed.

There are a number of microenterprise programs that can serve as models for your community. We share the stories of the Mountain Microenterprise Fund in western North Carolina and Nebraska's REAP program to get you started.

Mountain Microenterprise Fund

In the mountains of western North Carolina, Mountain Microenterprise Fund (MMF), a nonprofit organization, provides training, business loans and one-on-one counseling to micro entrepreneurs. Started in 1989, MMF has worked with almost 1,800 entrepreneurs and MMF alumni are operating about 900 businesses in the region. MMF's mission is to work with women, people of color, lower-income individuals, and rural people to help them realize their dreams of owning their own businesses. These businesses, in turn, help support the entrepreneurs, their families and their communities.

MMF's business training course, "Foundations," provides

entrepreneurs with "how to" information on starting or expanding a business. Entrepreneurs can take the 10-week course, three hours per week, at locations throughout the region. In 2002, almost 400 people graduated from Foundations. Once an entrepreneur has completed the training program, she can apply for a business loan of up to $25,000. These micro loans help bridge the capital gap for entrepreneurs who have difficulty getting loans through traditional sources such as banks.

What's innovative about MMF, however, is that they don't stop with business training and loans. MMF keeps alumni engaged through a membership program that offers entrepreneurs access to additional resources and networking opportunities. MMF also operates a for-profit enterprise, Mountain Made, in Asheville, North Carolina, that provides a retail outlet for western North Carolina artisans, one third of whom are alumni of MMF's Foundations program. As the staff at Mountain Made work with local artisans, they are able to identify their business development needs and, as appropriate, refer the artists to MMF for training, counseling or capital.

To learn more about Mountain Microenterprise, go to www.mtnmicro.org.

Nebraska's REAP

In rural Nebraska, where the primary employment source is self-employment, and the dominant business type is microenterprise (five or fewer employees), access to core business development services is critical. The Rural Enterprise Assistance Project (REAP) is meeting this challenge. REAP, a program of the private, nonprofit Center for Rural Affairs, is a microenterprise development program that works with start-up and existing small businesses throughout rural Nebraska. REAP is the largest microenterprise development program in Nebraska, rural or urban.

REAP continues to evolve and currently offers small business management training, networking, technical assistance, small loans, and loan packaging services to businesses. REAP uses a "dual delivery" system, offering both group and individual service options. In addition, the REAP Women's Business Center (WBC), the first in Nebraska, is reaching out to rural women entrepreneurs. The REAP WBC service center entered its fourth year in 2004. REAP uses business specialists located throughout the state to deliver WBC to other rural entrepreneurs.

Since 1990, REAP has provided services to more than 4,000 micro entrepreneurs, including 274 peer loans with an average loan size of $1,706. In 1998, REAP piloted the Direct Loan Program and in early 2000, it became a permanent part of REAP's loan services. The direct loan program makes individual loans of $1,000–$25,000 to entrepreneurs who have difficulty getting loans from any other sources.

One of REAP's new initiatives is providing services to the Hispanic/Latino community in rural Nebraska. Using USDA Rural Business Enterprise Grant (RBEG) funds, REAP established a rural Hispanic business development project, the REAP Hispanic Rural Business Center without walls (RH-RBC), in 2004. The Center will be piloted in three rural communities with an ultimate goal of providing business development services to rural Hispanic entrepreneurs statewide.

To learn more about the REAP program, go to www.cfra.org/reap.

ENTREPRENEURSHIP TRAINING AND BUSINESS COUNSELING PROGRAMS Aspiring and start-up entrepreneurs can often benefit from participation in training and counseling programs, either one-on-one or with other entrepreneurs. There are a number of well-tested "how to" training programs that take entrepreneurs through the process of starting their own businesses. While programs such as FastTrac and NxLevel are primarily for adult entrepreneurs, the Rural Entrepreneurship through Action Learning (REAL) curriculum serves youth as well as adults.

Counseling programs may be more appropriate for entrepreneurs who have already developed a business plan but need assistance with specific aspects of the business. For example, an entrepreneur might need help accessing export markets or understanding the licensing requirements for operating a commercial kitchen. These types of questions are best addressed through the services of a business counselor who works one-on-one with the entrepreneur.

Whatever training or counseling programs are used, you

should keep several things in mind as you create your strategy.

- Entrepreneurs need to be able to understand where to go to get these services so they don't become frustrated as they try to get help.
- Training and counseling programs should be user friendly. Aspiring and start-up entrepreneurs may still have their "day jobs" and need to be able to take a class or meet with a counselor in the evenings, on the weekends or even online.
- You need to know enough about an entrepreneur and her skills so that you can steer her toward the training program or business counselor that can best meet her needs.
- You need to remove barriers to participation so that as many entrepreneurs as possible can access these services. In response to the growing Hispanic population in North Carolina, REAL created Spanish REAL to meet the needs of this group of entrepreneurs.

The Spanish REAL Program

North Carolina REAL Enterprises has been providing entrepreneurship training in the state since the 1980s. Its programs are very well known and have served as models for effective entrepreneurship training around the world.

By the 1990s, REAL's basic training program (the REAL entrepreneurship class) was well established and was being utilized in a variety of settings and for a variety of populations. This period also coincided with a boom in Latino immigration into North Carolina. In fact, North Carolina's Hispanic population grew 395% over the course of the 1990s and Latinos now account for nearly 5% of the state's population. These new immigrants came to North Carolina in pursuit of opportunity and, for many, opportunity meant starting their own business.

While immigrants tend to start businesses at fast rates, they need the same help and assistance that others want before they start a new venture. But, in the case of new Latino immigrants, language proved to be a nearly insurmountable barrier. Since many spoke only Spanish, they could not access traditional programs offered in English. Recognizing this problem, NC REAL's leaders quickly translated their basic course into Spanish and began training bilingual facilitators.

In 2004, the Spanish REAL curriculum was in great demand and was offered in 23 counties across the state. As Latinos become more integrated into the local business community and more become interested in entrepreneurship, this level of activity is certain to grow. To learn more about Spanish REAL, go to www.ncreal.org.

FACILITATION AND COACHING An intensive and effective approach to working with aspiring and start-up entrepreneurs involves facilitation and coaching. In these approaches, individual coaches or facilitators identify entrepreneurs within their communities and work one-on-one with the entrepreneurs to help them access the resources they need to make sound decisions about getting into business and to growing a successful business once they begin the journey.

The pioneer in the field of Enterprise Facilitation™ is Ernesto Sirolli. Other forms of facilitation and coaching, such as the Kentucky Entrepreneurial Coaches Institute, are also being used. All these approaches have some commonalities. They are generally simple to create and execute. Facilitators and coaches must learn how to ask the right questions and connect entrepreneurs to resources, both inside and outside the community. This approach works best with entrepreneurs who are just getting started, those aspiring and start-up entrepreneurs who can benefit from the moral support that coaches and facilitators can provide. In addition, the effectiveness of these approaches is dependent on the people selected as facilitators and coaches. The quality of the assistance is driven by the skills, commitment and motivation of these support providers.

Kentucky Entrepreneurial Coaches Institute

Started in 2003, the Kentucky Entrepreneurial Coaches Institute (KECI) was designed to identify and train community leaders from a 19-county region in northeastern Kentucky to be effective entrepreneurial coaches. The program was launched in the most tobacco-dependent region in the state, with funding from the Kentucky Agricultural Development Board using tobacco settlement funds. The program was created in response to research that identified gaps in the entrepreneurial support struc-

RIPPLES FROM THE ZAMBEZI

If you are interested in learning more about Enterprise Facilitation™, we highly recommend Ernesto Sirolli's book, Ripples from the Zambezi. Ernesto shares stories from his journey developing the enterprise facilitation model. The stories from around the world will inspire your work with entrepreneurs in your community.

ture in the state. While Kentucky has service providers who can offer business counseling and other forms of assistance to entrepreneurs, there were few who served as coaches—listening, encouraging and connecting entrepreneurs to other entrepreneurs and specific types of technical assistance.

KECI provides volunteer community leaders with the skills they need to become effective coaches. In addition, the Institute is creating a network of coaches with strong personal connections so that they become a permanent part of the region's entrepreneurial support infrastructure. The first group of 30 coaches will complete their 15-month training in November 2005 and the second group will begin their journey in September 2005. Once completed, there will be 60 competent coaches volunteering their time and talent to help entrepreneurs in the region.

The community leaders participating in KECI come from all walks of life. Many have close ties to agriculture and are active community leaders. Some bring business experience to the program. Most importantly, they all have a willingness to be creative and think outside the box and a strong commitment to helping their communities and region by nurturing entrepreneurs.

The entrepreneurial coaches complement rather than compete with existing support providers. They are trained to ask tough questions, demand hard work and follow through by the entrepreneur and to network with local, regional and state service providers. They introduce entrepreneurs into the system of service providers rather than providing any direct assistance themselves.

To learn more about this innovative approach to entrepreneur support, go to www.uky.edu/Ag/KECI.

Strategies for Youth Entrepreneurs

The young people currently in your rural community may be your greatest resource for changing attitudes toward entrepreneurship and for creating new business ventures. However, we need to engage these youth, provide them with the skills and knowledge they need to be successful and support them as they develop and grow their ventures. National surveys of young people find that while many want to start their own businesses, few feel they have the skills to do so. What can you do?

A first step is to engage the youth in your community. Invite groups of students from the schools who have an interest in starting their own businesses and talk to them. Discover their dreams. Find out what ideas they have and what they are working on. Ask them what they need to make their dreams a reality, and then work with them to make this happen!

The next step is to use existing programs and models to build support for youth entrepreneurs:

- Networking can work for youth as well as for aspiring and start-up entrepreneurs by linking young entrepreneurs with experienced adult entrepreneurs who can mentor them.
- Education programs such as REAL and the National Federation for the Teaching of Entrepreneurship's BizTech can be brought to the schools and after-school programs in your community.
- Microenterprise programs can target youth.
- Business plan and other competitions can get youth engaged in putting their business ideas into a feasible plan.

There are resources and model programs for you to consider as you develop your strategy.

Youth Entrepreneurship Partnership

The Youth Entrepreneur Partnership (YEP), a program of the Nelson Institute in Nebraska, started in 2000 as a collaboration among a number of agencies in a nine-county rural region. YEP addresses four main aspects of entrepreneurial development among rural students: awareness and education, mentoring and apprenticeship, business training and leadership development. Two main components of the program are a career fair and an entrepreneurship curriculum. In its fourth year, the career fair brings an estimated 300 to 400 students to the McCook Community College Campus during spring break. Entrepreneurs are available to visit one-on-one with young people interested in emulating them.

The entrepreneurial curriculum, "Buzz on Biz," helps build skills by exposing young people to entrepreneurship as a viable career option. Started as an after school activity for 10th through 12th graders, Buzz on Biz is now available during the school day in three rural Nebraska high schools. When the YEP program is fully implemented, students in 8th through 12th grades will have opportunities to learn about entrepreneurship in their communities.

In addition to the career fair and the Buzz on Biz courses, YEP is developing an apprenticeship program. The apprenticeship component is also in the early stages of development. For this program, YEP has been chartered as an Explorer Post. This provides a leadership model for the students as well as mitigating potential liability issues.

Although in the early stages, YEP's goal to involve more young people in rural entrepreneurship could bring big payoffs to rural communities in the future.

Strategies for Growth-Oriented Entrepreneurs

Growth-oriented entrepreneurs have already made the commitment to grow their ventures. These entrepreneurs are already in business, so they've gotten through those difficult discovery and start-up stages. They are motivated to grow, which often means developing a new product or cultivating a new market. Their support needs are moving from more general forms of assistance to very specific, targeted business information needs.

To effectively support these growth-oriented entrepreneurs, our support services must focus on:

- Customized assistance
- Higher order assistance
- Peer support and networking
- Expanding/strengthening the management team

CUSTOMIZED ASSISTANCE As the growth-oriented entrepreneur's needs become more targeted and specific, the support we provide must evolve as well. A growth-oriented entrepreneur will not be well served by sitting through a 12-week class in how to start a business. Customized assistance is provided one-on-one in response to very specific questions from the entrepreneur. The service provider might provide market research to help the entrepreneur better understand a new market. A university textile lab might develop a prototype product for a manufacturing entrepreneur to market to prospective customers. This assistance is designed to respond to the needs of the entrepreneur as they actively grow the business.

Kentucky Highlands Investment Corporation

Kentucky Highlands Investment Corporation (KHIC) is an economic development organization that uses the tools of debt and equity capital to create jobs and wealth in a nine-county region of southeastern Kentucky. This "capital led" strategy has evolved, leading to the creation of a sustainable model for entrepreneurial development in one of the poorest rural regions in the country. KHIC was founded in 1968—one of the original community development corporations funded by the federal government. Over time, KHIC has become what we call an "entrepreneurial support organization" (ESO), with some important lessons for those seeking to create specialized organizations to support entrepreneurship.

- LESSON ONE

KHIC focuses on the entrepreneur and her needs, not the business. In addition to putting together a financing package that works best for the entrepreneur, KHIC also provides the assistance needed for success. This assistance may be as simple as identifying marketing support for the entrepreneur or as complex as having a KHIC staff person work side-by-side with the entrepreneur for a year to turn a struggling business around.

- LESSON TWO

KHIC staff members are well qualified (many are entrepreneurs) and have a strong commitment to the region. Deep roots in the region help to keep staff focused on the mission of KHIC. They also work hard to help struggling entrepreneurs rather than simply writing off the investment.

- LESSON THREE

KHIC is creative and aggressive in tapping grants, state and federal resources to support the overall mission. These funds help the organization provide sustainable assistance and financing to the region's entrepreneurs.

- LESSON FOUR

A single ESO is unlikely to have a major long-term impact in a region unless it partners with others to create a culture of entrepreneurship. KHIC's success over time encouraged the development of other entrepreneurial support organizations and helped to create a more entrepreneurial region. These partner-ships also allow each ESO to focus on those entrepreneurs they can support most effectively—KHIC works with existing entrepreneurs whose needs are more sophisticated while other organizations focus on micro entrepreneurs.

KHIC has a long history in its region and benefited from strong federal support in its early years. However, the lessons learned can be applied to your efforts to create effective support organizations for entrepreneurs in your communities.

To learn more about KHIC, go to www.khic.org. You can also read a more detailed case study of KHIC on the RUPRI Center's website, www.ruraleship.org.

HIGHER ORDER ASSISTANCE General practice attorneys and business counselors may be qualified to help a start-up entrepreneur with legal or financial questions. However, as we begin to support growth-oriented entrepreneurs, higher order services may be required. The growth-oriented entrepreneur who is developing a new product may need a patent attorney. A rapid-ly growing entrepreneur may need the capital and expertise that a venture capitalist can provide. If these services are not available locally, we need to develop a network of external service providers, often in nearby urban areas that can be tapped to help these growth-oriented entrepreneurs.

PEER SUPPORT AND NETWORKING Whether you tar-get aspiring, start-up or growth-oriented entrepreneurs, the importance of peer support and networking doesn't change. The sophistication of the network may increase as the entrepreneurs actively pursue new opportunities for growth. The "front porch network" may give rise to a more formalized network like the Council for Entrepreneurial Development.

Entrepreneurial League System®

Entrepreneurs are made, not born. This belief is at the heart of the Entrepreneurial League System® (ELS) developed by Tom Lyons and Gregg Lichtenstein. ELS is based on two assump-tions—successful entrepreneurship requires a set of skills and no two entrepreneurs have the same skill set. Most importantly, an entrepreneur's skill set can be developed over time, making ELS a model for human capital development rather than simply business development.

Using the baseball farm system as a model, ELS is organized into leagues, moving from Rookie to Single A, Double A, Triple A and the Major Leagues. Based on an assessment of their skills, entrepreneurs are placed into a league level and provided with assistance to develop their skills and enable them to move up through the system. Service providers are also organized into league levels, matching their services to the specific types of entrepreneurs they can most effectively help. For example, micro loan providers might work with Rookie and Single A entrepreneurs while venture capital investors might work with Major Leaguers.

The ELS system provides benefits to entrepreneurs, service providers and the community or region. For entrepreneurs, the system provides a very clear path to success—it is clear how to enter the system, what skills you need to develop and what resources are available to do so. For service providers, the system works because it directs entrepreneurs to the service providers who are best equipped to help them. And for the community or region, ELS offers an opportunity to support entrepreneurship at a scale that can truly transform the region.

So, how is ELS working on the ground? The most significant implementation of ELS is occurring in the Advantage Valley region of West Virginia. This multi-county region includes both urban and rural places, providing a good test for the ELS model. Advantage Valley began recruiting entrepreneurs in the fall of 2004 with a goal of having 48 entrepreneurs organized into Rookie, Single A, Double A and Triple A teams. Anecdotally, we know that ELS makes sense to entrepreneurs. Advantage Valley ELS has received significant foundation support to fully implement the model so keep a watch on West Virginia!

To learn more about ELS in West Virginia, go to www.advantagevalleyels.com.

EXPANDING/STRENGTHENING THE MANAGEMENT TEAM An entrepreneur on her own may work fine in the early stages of starting a business. Growth-oriented entrepreneurs, however, often begin to face constraints on their ability to manage a growing enterprise. A part-time bookkeeper might work well for a start-up, but a growing venture may need a chief financial officer. The entrepreneur may be able to manage employees when the business is family run but a growing venture may need a human resources director. Building this new management team can often be a challenge for entrepreneurs. It's hard to share power in an organization, especially one you have built from the ground up. However, it's even harder to be successful without an experienced entrepreneurial team. These entrepreneurs need help recognizing their staffing needs and finding the right people to fill those needs. For example, Kentucky Highlands helped one of their entrepreneurs find a CFO, even to the point of conducting interviews and recommending candidates.

The more sophisticated needs of growth-oriented entrepreneurs require different entrepreneurship development strategies. Two models, HomeTown Competitiveness and Economic Gardening, offer different approaches to supporting growth entrepreneurs.

HomeTown Competitiveness

HomeTown Competitiveness (HTC) is a comprehensive approach to long-term rural community sustainability. This approach goes beyond the traditional tunnel vision of economic development. HTC helps the community focus on four interrelated strategies that depend on each other for ultimate success.

The first and most important strategy is to build a skilled and increasingly inclusive leadership group with the capacity to improve and sustain the community. The second strategy is to engage and attract youth and young families. The third strategy is to act now to capture a portion of the wealth that will transfer between generations. And, the fourth strategy is to use the transferred wealth to energize and support entrepreneurs to build local businesses and create jobs.

The steps in the HTC process mirror what we've been talking about throughout this guide—determining readiness, making the case, assessing your community, developing targeted strategies, and implementing your plans. Let's focus here on how strategies were targeted to specific types of entrepreneurial talent in the HTC model.

HTC was piloted in 2002 in Ord, Nebraska, rural Valley County—population 5,000. Ord is rural by anyone's definition, located over two hours from the nearest Interstate. While visiting entrepreneurs in Ord as part of the assessment process, the local leadership team discovered something remarkable—at least 10–15 entrepreneurs with growth potential and motivation! The team also identified a number of Main Street businesses that were grappling with (or soon would be) how to transfer their businesses to a new generation of entrepreneurs and keep the businesses in Valley County. This visitation process gave the leadership in Ord a target for strategy development—growth-oriented entrepreneurs and business transfers.

Armed with these targets, the leadership team began to develop strategies to help these entrepreneurs, including more customized assistance by service providers. In the years since HTC was piloted in Ord, a number of good things have happened. The town has a strategic set of goals for economic development and is focused on those entrepreneurs who can have a real impact on the local economy. Both youth and adults have participated in the new leadership program that is now institutionalized in the community. The goal of retaining at least 5% of future wealth transfer has been exceeded. Most importantly, the people of Ord are actively engaged in the process of revitalizing their community and are hopeful about the future.

For more information on the HTC model, go to www.ruraleship.org.

Economic Gardening

The seeds of economic gardening were sown in Littleton, Colorado, in 1987. With a new director of economic development, Chris Gibbons, and several thousand laid off employees from the community's major manufacturer, the city pioneered an alternative to the traditional economic development practice of hunting for new industry. City officials decided to grow their own jobs through entrepreneurship rather than trying to recruit jobs into the community. The approach was to build the economy from the inside by nurturing and growing entrepreneurs—the concept of economic gardening was born!

In Littleton, the focus of their economic gardening efforts is on high growth companies—those few companies that can really drive a local economy. Knowing that these companies do well in an environment where information and innovation flow freely, the city focuses on the following:

- PROVIDING INFORMATION Entrepreneurs located in Littleton have access to a wealth of information provided at no or limited cost by the city. An entrepreneur can have a marketing list developed or have an analyst produce a report on industry trends using any of the many databases or thousands of publications the city can access. Another entrepreneur may use Geographic Information Systems (GIS) software to map customer addresses. Access to information is vital for new entrepreneurs who may not have the resources to hire marketing experts or to develop the internal capacity to process such information. The city, in essence, becomes part of each entrepreneur's team.

- INVESTING IN INFRASTRUCTURE Like most cities and towns, Littleton invests in basic physical infrastructure such as streets, sidewalks and water systems. As part of economic gardening, however, the city also invests in infrastructure that's important to entrepreneurs—quality of life investments like recreation and open space, great schools and festivals. And, they invest in "intellectual infrastructure"— training programs, connections to higher education institutions and other means of keeping the skills of the community's entrepreneurs sharp and their businesses competitive.

- MAKING CONNECTIONS Leaders in Littleton believe that entrepreneurs need to connect to other entrepreneurs to stay on the cutting edge. So, the city facilitates linkages to trade associations, other companies, universities and think tanks where entrepreneurs can network and be exposed to new forms of innovation.

Economic gardening provides an effective set of support services targeted to growth entrepreneurs in Littleton. Can it work as well in your rural community as it does in the city of Littleton? Remember, there's no silver bullet! However, the concepts behind economic gardening—growing your own, targeting assistance to specific entrepreneurial types, and providing information, infrastructure and connections—can be applied in communities of all sizes.

For more information on economic gardening, go to www.littletongov.org/bia.

Strategies for Entrepreneurial Growth Companies

Entrepreneurial growth companies are fast growing and innovative. They have tapped into new markets, developed new products and are using new business models. They may be home-grown, like Cabela's, or the entrepreneur may have come to rural America to be closer to family, natural amenities or a quieter lifestyle. Whatever the reason, entrepreneurial growth companies in your midst should be nurtured and supported, but in different ways.

Entrepreneurs operating these high growth companies often have the skills and the management team needed to grow the business. What they may require is support from the external environment:

- Room to expand the business to a new and larger building or site.
- Access to capital, both debt and equity, and the ability to develop a relationship with financial advisors in the community or region.
- Quality workforce both in terms of employees and management with the skills required by the growing business.
- Quality infrastructure, both traditional physical and high-tech telecommunications infrastructure, as well as quality of life infrastructure, such as good schools, recreation facilities and natural areas.
- Willingness on the part of the community to listen and respond to the needs so that issues can be resolved quickly and collaboratively.

These entrepreneurial growth companies are best served by the higher order support systems we described earlier.

Investing in Entrepreneurship Strategies

Now that we've described how to target strategies by entrepreneurial type, you might want to work through an exercise of investing in these alternative strategies. Using what you learned through the assessment and targeting process, use the following ECONOMIC DEVELOPMENT INVESTMENT EXERCISE to begin to develop the set of programs that will make up your entrepreneurship development strategy. Use the team you put in place for the assessment process and work through the following exercise. Try to come to consensus on where your dollars are best spent to achieve results.

Economic Development Investment Exercise

Assume your community or organization has $100,000 a year for three years to invest in strategies to energize local entrepreneurs. How would you invest these funds? The following are some options you might consider.

ECONOMIC DEVELOPMENT INVESTMENT EXERCISE

MICRO Develop or expand a local microenterprise program.	MENTORS & PEER GROUPS Develop a mentor or peer group program.	ENTREPRENEURSHIP EDUCATION Offer entrepreneurship classes to K-12 students and adults.
FACILITATION Provide entrepreneurs with coaching or facilitation services.	TRAINING Provide area access to entrepreneurial training workshops.	INCENTIVES Provide local business incentives.
COUNSELING Support business counseling services for local entrepreneurs including one-on-one technical assistance such as feasibility studies and business plans.	THERE ARE MANY CHOICES – THE CHALLENGE IS INVESTING IN THOSE OPTIONS THAT GET RESULTS AND BUILD CAPACITY.	TECHNICAL ASSISTANCE Create access to technical assistance including legal, accounting, marketing, management, human resources, and other business skill areas.
NETWORKS Develop networking infrastructure for entrepreneurs.	INFRASTRUCTURE Ensure solid business infrastructure.	MARKET DEVELOPMENT Provide assistance to help entrepreneurs develop new markets.
OTHER? Are there other strategies that you feel would be a great investment?	INVESTMENT CAPITAL Increase access to investment capital for entrepreneurs.	INCUBATORS Develop a local or area incubator and program for local entrepreneurs.

Elements of Successful Practice

We like to say, "It's the practice, not the form" when we talk about entrepreneurship development strategies. What we mean is that it matters less whether you choose to support growth-oriented entrepreneurs through an incubator strategy or through customized assistance at the Small Business Development Center. What really matters is how you put into practice the strategies you choose.

By observing successful entrepreneurship strategies since 1999, we've discovered the following elements of successful practice:

- ENTREPRENEUR FOCUSED The strategy focuses on the entrepreneur and what he needs to be successful. It is as much a human resource development challenge as it is about creating new ventures.

- COMMUNITY BASED Successful strategies have strong and broad support within the community. The community is committed to creating an entrepreneurial environment in which entrepreneurs can be nurtured and grow.

- ASSET-BASED APPROACH Strategies grow out of a thorough understanding of the assets available in the community to support entrepreneurs and an assessment of the types and needs of entrepreneurs.

- STRATEGICALLY TARGETED Recognizing that resources are limited, successful strategies target specific types of entrepreneurs based on the initial assessment and the development goals in the community.

- ACCESS TO RESOURCES The strategy builds on local assets but also taps external resources to provide the support that entrepreneurs need.

- PROVISION OF THE BASICS Successful programs insure that basic services, particularly networks, are provided to entrepreneurs.

Just as importantly, we have seen entrepreneurship strategies fail when they:

- STRESS THE FORM OVER THE FUNCTION Incubators that are little more than real estate developments will not provide the type of support needed to nurture entrepreneurs.

- LACK OF FOCUS Programs are not successful when they try to meet the need of different types of entrepreneurs with standardized "one size fits all" programs.

- LACK OF STAYING POWER AND RESOURCES It takes time to support and nurture an entrepreneur. If support programs lack funding and resources, they are unlikely to be around to help the entrepreneur when the next crisis arises.

- FAILURE TO CONSIDER THE NEED TO CHANGE THE CULTURE AND ENVIRONMENT If we don't work to create a supportive culture in rural America for entrepreneurs, support programs may well fail to achieve the desired outcomes.

Additional Resources

More information is available on the E^2 *Energizing Entrepreneurs* website at www.energizingentrepreneurs.org. Once there, click on "Strategies" to find resources that support the information in this chapter.

As part of the RUPRI Center's training materials, we have developed an *Entrepreneurial Pathways* series. Each *Pathway* provides more detailed information on strategies that you can use to support aspiring and start-ups, growth-oriented, youth, and business transfers. You'll find more information on the *Entrepreneurial Pathways* series by going to www.energizingentrepreneurs.org.

There are many sources of information on the strategies

we've described in this chapter. To help you get started, we recommend the following:

For information on networking check out *Building Entrepreneurial Networks* by the National Commission on Entrepreneurship. This book includes case studies of some premier networking organizations including the Council for Entrepreneurial Development.

For information on microenterprise, the Association for Enterprise Opportunity is the trade association for microenterprise associations. They provide information and training that is very useful to both new and experienced organizations. www.microenterpriseworks.org

For information on incubators, the National Business Incubation Association is the trade association for organizations involved in business incubation. They offer training and information resources to their members. www.nbia.org

For information on youth entrepreneurship, the Consortium for Entrepreneurship Education (www.entre-ed.org), REAL Enterprises (www.realenterprises.org) and the National Foundation for Teaching Entrepreneurship (www.nfte.com) all provide information on curriculum, standards, and innovative programs to expose youth in your communities to entrepreneurship.

A good overall publication on rural entrepreneurship strategies is "Building New Economies in Rural America," the proceedings from the *Tools for Entrepreneurship Conference* sponsored by the Appalachian Regional Commission. The publication is available online at http://www.arc.gov/index.do?nodeId=1135.

CHAPTER 9
BUILDING CAPACITY
FOR ENTREPRENEURSHIP
DEVELOPMENT

The Tupelo Miracle

The story of Tupelo, Mississippi, is often referred to as a "miracle" because the poorest county in the U.S. in 1940 became the second wealthiest county in Mississippi in the 1990s. The Tupelo story is one of capacity building. In the 1930s, Tupelo and Lee County, Mississippi, had no competitive advantage—the agricultural base was in decline, and the industrial base was almost nonexistent; physical infrastructure was limited; the town and county were isolated; and the population was primarily illiterate. Through the leadership of a civic entrepreneur, George McLean, Tupelo embarked on a different approach to economic development than other parts of the south. Rejecting strategies that focused on luring companies with offers of cheap, unskilled labor and incentives, the leaders in Tupelo instead focused on developing the human resources in the region as the basis for economic development. They argued that a strong community leads to a strong economy.

A number of principles guided the development process in Tupelo, and these are also relevant to communities considering entrepreneurship development:

- People in the community must be responsible for addressing local problems, and developing this human resource is the first step in the development process.
- Leadership is important, but you also have to develop the organizations and institutions that will implement the development strategy.

- The development process must be both local and regional to achieve its fullest impact.
- Any development process must have broad-based participation by all members of the community, starting with the poorest members.
- Communities must build on their assets, the most important of which are people.

The evolution of the Tupelo community included such initiatives as the creation of rural development councils to bring programs to the rural parts of the county, the development of incubators and worker training programs, and upgrading the education infrastructure through the creation of a community college and the addition of a University of Mississippi campus in the region. To learn more about the Tupelo story, we recommend Tupelo: The Evolution of a Community, written by Vaughn Grisham Jr. and published by the Kettering Foundation.

What is Community Capacity?

As we have worked with communities nationwide, we've established a very basic definition of community capacity. We like to say that community capacity is the knowledge, the skills and the attitudes necessary to improve and sustain your community. It's important to have a good working definition of this since we don't want to limit the term to mean just a good core of experienced leaders, or a strong local government staff or even one or two really active service clubs. Capacity is a more inclusive term and the dimensions of knowledge, skills and attitudes can be considered in this way:

- KNOWLEDGE An understanding of the past (heritage), of current conditions and future trends. A good example is the knowledge that your community's economy was built by someone locally who started off as an entrepreneur.

- SKILLS Group process techniques such as giving and receiving information, making decisions, managing conflict. Engaging the rest of the community in a town hall meeting to discuss ways to support local entrprepreneurs is an example of how those skills work together.

- ATTITUDES An open and curious approach to new ideas and approaches and an understanding that change can be useful. Making the change from industrial recruitment strategies to a focus on entrepreneurship is an example of this capacity.

Other definitions of community capacity can be useful, too. You may have come across the notion of "social capital" as a way to describe the capacity of a community to improve and sustain itself. Social capital centers on the health and vigor of societies and communities. In simple terms, it refers to the networks, trust and reciprocal relationships that keep communities working smoothly and for the benefit of all. In the same way that leadership skills can be learned, social capital can be built. In central Louisiana, for example, the Rapides Foundation created a program to recruit and train local leaders from several parishes. The program helped leaders assess their own community's social capital, and develop strategies for building on their local knowledge, skills and attitudes.

According to sociologist John Allen, there are two types of social capital—"bridging" and "conserving." As the words suggest, bridging social capital equates with strong networking infrastructure that is actively being used by community residents. Such communities are typically more productive, progressive and dynamic. Conversely, conserving social capital (while it has many desirable qualities such as the preservation of traditions) can restrict the ability of the community to undertake necessary change. Communities dominated by conserving social capital tend to be insular and parochial.

Why is social capital or community capacity so important to energizing rural entrepreneurs? There are at least two answers to this question. First, societies and communities with high social capital are also communities that produce stable environments for living and commerce, as well as higher quality of life. Communities rich in social capital are often communities rich with assets in the arts, recreation, education and entertainment. They are places where entrepreneurs want to live, start, and grow their enterprises. Second, these places exhibit the capacity or ability to act on challenges and opportunities. Communities with active and strong capacity are effectively addressing a wide range of issues from housing to poverty to economic development. These communities are more likely to be proactive about embracing the opportunity to grow through entrepreneurship.

Research by the Kauffman Foundation (and others) strongly suggests that entrepreneurs need contact with other entrepreneurs and mentors, and access to resources and expertise. This research also suggests that the likely pathway for entrepreneurs to meet these needs is through networking. Networking is based on relationships between people and their institutions. There are many forms of relationships, but we are concerned with viable and trusting relationships that enable collaboration to occur.

The more a community is networked and the more the networks are used, the greater the strength and quality of the networking infrastructure. There must be strong networking within the community and effective networks that link the community with the larger world. External networking enables a community to broaden its learning and collaboration opportunities beyond the finite assets of the community itself. Communites with strong networking infrastructure not only create desirable places to live, they also have the capacity to employ that infrastructure to help entrepreneurs address their special needs.

If communities with strong social capital can evolve supportive entrepreneurial environments, then how do communities build the social capital they need to encourage entrepreneurship? Clearly, community capacity-building experience is central to answering this question. On the flip side, can we build entrepreneurial places without strong social capital and entrepreneurial social infrastructure? More research must be done, but it appears likely that efforts to energize entrepreneurship in places with weak capacity and conserving social capital may have limited success.

Process and Strategies for Increasing Capacity

Communities with high levels of capacity use a systematic process for working toward community improvement. Lots of small towns engage in a strategic planning process or create a comprehensive land use plan that includes community goals. Even those engaged in historic preservation use a process that indicates the creation of this capacity. In each case, a core group gets started by setting some goals, perhaps developing a vision statement, selecting strategies and then implementing some type of effort. The project may change but the process is strikingly similar and, in almost every case, the focus is on some type of community improvement.

What happens when a community group goes through such a systematic process? In the best situations, individual citizens learn skills, clubs and organizations are strengthened and made more efficient, and information about the present and the future is spread throughout the community. This is evidence of building capacity to improve and sustain the community, because it means that the knowledge, skills and attitudes are in place to deal with future opportunities and challenges. A volunteer who learns how to lead a group discussion as part of a community improvement project can then take those skills to a chamber forum with entrepreneurs in the community. The capacity level of the entire community is raised.

Increased capacity among the citizens participating in a community improvement project is one of the best rationales for encouraging widespread participation. Obviously, the more residents that take part in the process, the more residents gain skills and experiences that can be applied to future projects. However, there are other reasons why public participation is so important to building local capacity. At the most basic level, a steering committee or core group must be representative of the community at large in order to insure that once goals, strategies and plans are articulated, the community will accept and implement those plans. If a small group of "in-crowd" power brokers makes all the decisions and then announces the changes, there's no way to guarantee acceptance. And the lack of acceptance ultimately means failure, whether it's a bond issue that doesn't pass, or a new tax that's voted down, or an entrepreneurship education program that doesn't get funded. Public involvement is much like an insurance policy for support and implementation. In small towns where volunteers are so very important to getting anything done, lack of involvement in the planning phase might mean there's nobody around to help take action and really do something.

It's also true that, in addition to the very practical aspect of insuring acceptance, public participation is what really makes democracy work. Our small towns are the very laboratories where our democracy is rebuilt every day with systems of checks, balances and active citizens that control the future of their town. While it may sound idealistic, this type of public participation is really the foundation of our way of life.

So, how does community capacity link to entrepreneurship? Clifton, Illinois, provides a good illustration. Local leaders and business people are proud of their school system, recreation facilities and health care strategies. They also use these public assets to attract private investment. Local farmers are part of the town's leadership and entrepreneurship pool. When retail sales began to decline, business owners dug into their own pockets to improve sidewalks and provide better access for its older citizens. The local business association published a brochure highlighting all that Clifton had to offer, and signage for a community calendar was erected in the city park.

Communities with strong capacity can create a seamless and very intentional atmosphere and system of support for local entrepreneurs and even develop a specialized organization that facilitates support for entrepreneurs. Within this environment, local entrepreneurs and others will work together to evolve a culture of entrepreneurship. To make this link between capacity and entrepreneurship, we need to start by assessing community capacity.

Assessing Community Capacity

We've developed a basic questionnaire that can be used to discover strengths and weaknesses in community capacity. You can find this helpful tool—the **Community Capacity Questionnaire—at the end of the chapter on page 145**. Here are a few ideas on how the questionnaire might be used.

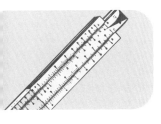

- Have individuals complete the survey during a service club or chamber of commerce meeting and discuss the results at the next meeting. Remember, your results will reflect the opinions of participants only and not the entire community. The survey is for discussion purposes only!
- Mail the survey to a much larger group and use the responses as the basis for a series of newspaper articles to spark conversations within the community. This can generate good discussion topics for a range of community meetings.
- Use the survey with different age groups and compare the results, for example, between high school students and senior citizens. Then bring the two groups together for a conversation.

You can close all of these sessions by identifying the two or three most important areas for improvement. Then you should take all the input received from the survey and use it for some thoughtful planning on how to improve the capacity of the community. Check back to Chapter 6 on Readiness for more ideas.

Strategies for Sustaining Capacity

It's an old community development adage that a crisis or sense of urgency will be very, very helpful in getting a community organized and energized but the hardest part is keeping things going. The communities that are most successful are, of course, the ones that are persistent and don't let participation and interest dwindle. But how exactly does that happen?

We think the real keys to maintaining momentum are leadership development and youth engagement. Let's explore both of those topics as well as some specific strategies that will help you keep interest high with results over the long term.

Leadership Development

There are certainly many different ways to address the need for leadership in a community. In fact, one of our tried and true group training activities is to ask folks to "Think of a leader that you have known personally. What made that person memorable?"

It may be a teacher or a coach or sometimes even a supervisor who is remembered, but the list of leadership characteristics is almost always the same: dedicated, hard working, visionary, good communicator, fair, competent, honest, good at managing conflict, open to new ideas, able to delegate and share power . . . the list goes on because we all have very high expectations of our leaders! However, it's also true that most of these skills can be learned, improved and practiced. It really makes the case for community leadership programs.

Having a regular program in a community that identifies and supports leadership skills can be a tremendous asset to building capacity. Leadership programs come in many varieties. The best ones are skill-based and include some type of project activity as part of the program. Really effective leadership development does more than just create connections among residents. One of the most important impacts that results from a community leadership program is the systematic way that newcomers and residents of all types are encouraged to take on leadership roles. It also means addressing ethnic and racial diversity in a systematic, recognized fashion rather than simply ignoring changes in population. Diversity in the leadership of a community is a sign of strength, vitality and increasing capacity to deal with change. It should be a goal for every community.

Just as we describe community capacity in terms of knowledge, skills and attitudes, so too can leadership development address those very same dimensions. Leadership does require specialized knowledge of the community, special skills for working with groups and individuals and certainly positive attitudes about change, resources and the future.

For entrepreneurship development to occur, you should consider how to engage entrepreneurs in leadership positions. Entrepreneurs are often so focused on their businesses that they don't seek out leadership roles. You need to come to them! Encouraging an entrepreneur to become chair of the chamber's new entrepreneur committee or to facilitate an entrepreneurial network may be a great way to introduce them to other leadership roles in the community. Remember, first engage them in something where their passion lies!

Youth Engagement

Many communities are successful in building capacity by targeting youth and young families for inclusion in community improvement efforts. Two of the tried and true strategies for getting results are mentoring relationships and variations on the theme of internships.

Mentoring a newcomer, emerging leader or young entrepreneur offers benefits to both sides of the relationship. The mentor gets to share and reflect on their experience and the mentored gets the confidence building help they need. Many communities have leaders that develop these kinds of relationships out of habit or good will rather than through a formalized program. However, a chamber of commerce or service club could establish a program that matches up partners of differing ages and experiences. For example, seasoned entrepreneurs might work with someone just starting up an enterprise, or work with high school students in a school-based enterprise. Whether it's structured or informal, mentoring relationships offer a lot toward building community capacity. And, entrepreneurs tell us that it's very helpful to talk with someone who has "been there, done that."

Another good strategy is the use of various types of internships. High school students can become interns in local businesses even for short periods of time to learn about entrepreneurship. Nonprofits and local government can also make great use of intern placements and shouldn't be limited to just the high school. Many community colleges and universities offer programs that place interns with real world entrepreneurs to gain valuable work experience and see role models in action. This offers a pathway for the student to learn about entrepreneurship and become connected to the community.

Strategies for Maintaining Momentum

Suppose your community decides to focus on identifying and supporting local entrepreneurs. You've had some discussions, found a champion or two, done some assessments, organized a group, and even developed a plan. All of that took a lot of energy and now your progress seems to be faltering a bit. What do you do now?

It's certainly not uncommon for the interest and energy in many groups to wane after all the work in getting started and developing a plan together has been accomplished. This is the time to consider some of these strategies to keep the momentum going.

FOCUS ON VISIBILITY How many people in town really know what your group is doing? Does the effort have enough visibility to keep people interested and accountable? Frankly, if nobody in town knows about your plans for supporting entrepreneurs, then why should any of the volunteers follow through on their assignments? Visibility is achieved through newspaper articles, presentations at service clubs, and items on the city council agenda—any way that the public can be made aware of your efforts.

DEVELOP A PUBLIC RELATIONS MESSAGE Make sure that your entrepreneurship support team has a positive image within the community. If your group is known as the one that gets things done and has a good time, you'll find it easier to recruit volunteers. Highlight the entrepreneurs that you've supported and recruit them to help you build this positive image. Use that vision statement you spent time crafting as often as possible to identify your efforts and keep everyone focused on the outcomes. Sometimes a logo on a t-shirt or a ball cap can help establish the identity of the group and help everyone feel a part of your team.

CELEBRATE YOUR PROGRESS This may be part of public relations but it's so important that it deserves special mention. Nothing motivates people like the celebration of progress. Small wins are important, and being inventive about how to celebrate each step toward a goal is an important part of maintaining momentum. Celebrations can range from ribbon-cuttings and parades for local entrepreneurs to an "Entrepreneur Day" in the schools and community. Use the local school for a supply of artists and musicians to make an ordinary event more special (and attract parents and grandparents to see their students perform.)

AWARD AND REWARD   In addition to celebrations for group achievements, be sure to reward individual efforts. Some volunteers like plaques, but other ways to reward hard work can be gift certificates for local merchants (support those local entrepreneurs!) or scholarships for entrepreneurship workshops or conferences where the volunteer can represent the community. Some service clubs will select a member of the year and waive dues for that person—a small reward but it's the recognition that keeps a person working as a volunteer. Award programs can be important, too, in keeping the community aware of a project and in securing support in the long run. A community business plan competition can generate a real buzz around your efforts. Selecting an "Entrepreneur of the Year" for your community brings attention to the entrepreneur and to your program.

ASK FOR FEEDBACK   Nothing can be more stirring to a group gone stagnant than the chance to evaluate what's gone well and what's gone wrong. An evaluation of the organization by its members can take the form of a discussion (you might brainstorm likes, dislikes and ideas for change) or even a paper and pencil survey that rates the organization. The important thing here is to regain some momentum by piquing the interest of the members and engaging them in problem-solving about how to improve and get back on track.

GET OFFICIAL ENDORSEMENTS   Got a new mayor or council member? Get an official endorsement of your project effort and make a big deal of it with a photo and a news story. An official endorsement can restart a lagging effort just by getting some attention. If you want people in your town to notice and support entrepreneurs, try establishing an official "entrepreneur month" and organizing some activities along that theme with special endorsements from local officials.

PROJECT THE IMAGE OF AN ENTREPRENEURIAL COMMUNITY   How do you project the image that your town wants/needs/supports entrepreneurs? Run newspaper stories on local entrepreneurs and their business starts. Feature a high school class that comes up with potential business ideas. Offer a workshop on entrepreneurship topics and feature local entrepreneurs—get the local cable channel to televise it. Think about ways to make your town one that's really known for supporting entrepreneurs. Any of these activities will create some momentum and jumpstart a project that has run down. Consider it as marketing and "branding" for your community.

Perhaps the most important technique in building capacity and maintaining momentum is to start small and to be persistent. Do SOMETHING! In Shenandoah, Iowa, one entrepreneur opened up his house and front porch to host an informal, ongoing discussion among existing and potential entrepreneurs. Suddenly there was a place to go and people who were interested. In Chadron, Nebraska, one group of community leaders just got together once a month to brainstorm "Wild Ideas" about community improvement. Gradually, their conversations developed into projects. In St. Paris, Ohio, several entrepreneurs got together at the local cafe to act as a support group for one another because there was no other source of inspiration or ideas. In Lincoln County, Kansas, regional planning organizations made the decision to become an Internet provider and invested in a T-1 line that's made the organization financially stable and brought electronic commerce to the county. Building capacity comes in all levels, informal and formal, spontaneous and structured, but can't be ignored if you want success in the long term.

And remember—start small . . . be persistent . . . get others involved.

Please circle the appropriate number for each statement.
1 *Never* 2 *Very seldom* 3 *Occasionally* 4 *Some of the time* 5 *All of the time*

Community Capacity

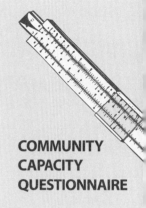

COMMUNITY CAPACITY QUESTIONNAIRE

1. Community leaders understand and use information (such as the US Census) about the community and the region to make strategic decisions. 1 2 3 4 5

2. Pride in our community shows up in neighborhood and community beautification efforts. 1 2 3 4 5

3. People from different backgrounds and incomes work together to make the community a better place. 1 2 3 4 5

4. Organizations (service clubs) and institutions (hospitals, schools, churches) in our community work together. 1 2 3 4 5

5. We believe that, in the long run, we have to do it ourselves. 1 2 3 4 5

6. Residents in our community have many chances to participate in decision making. 1 2 3 4 5

7. Our community leaders and organizations encourage a deliberate transition of power to a younger generation. 1 2 3 4 5

8. The community supports a leadership development training program. 1 2 3 4 5

9. The community provides leadership opportunities for youth. 1 2 3 4 5

10. In our community, women and minorities are accepted in all types of leadership roles. 1 2 3 4 5

11. Strong multi-generational family traditions are demonstrated in our community when we see all ages participating in events. 1 2 3 4 5

12. Our traditional institutions (schools, churches, businesses, etc.) are action oriented and responsive to the needs of the people who live here. 1 2 3 4 5

13. New residents typically feel welcome in our community. 1 2 3 4 5

14. The community demonstrates a willingness to seek help from the outside. 1 2 3 4 5

COMMUNITY CAPACITY QUESTIONNAIRE

(continued)

15. Our community projects show respect for the various cultures of community members. 1 2 3 4 5

16. Typically, our leaders build on the positive things in our community rather than focusing on the things that are wrong. 1 2 3 4 5

17. Residents in our community tolerate others with different perspectives. 1 2 3 4 5

18. As we work on community issues, we welcome questions, alternatives and make use of research-based evidence. 1 2 3 4 5

19. In our community projects, "who does what by when" (accountability) is made public. 1 2 3 4 5

20. Lots of different people take on leadership roles. 1 2 3 4 5

21. We pay attention to the results of our community betterment efforts by celebrating successes while acknowledging that there is still work to do. 1 2 3 4 5

22. We keep improving community projects by using some reflection time to understand what works and what doesn't. 1 2 3 4 5

23. A variety of people will run for public office and feel that doing so is not a risk. 1 2 3 4 5

Local Economy

24. Our business community offers high quality on a regular basis. 1 2 3 4 5

25. Members of the community and local businesses are aware of competitive positioning (marketing, global niche, etc.). 1 2 3 4 5

26. The community supports an active economic development program. 1 2 3 4 5

27. People in our community recognize the value of supporting local business. 1 2 3 4 5

28. The economic development program strategically targets resources for the best return on the dollar. 1 2 3 4 5

29. The community is supportive of entrepreneurship in media, the press and other areas. 1 2 3 4 5

30. The schools and youth groups provide opportunities for youth to learn about entrepreneurship.   1 2 3 4 5

31. The community leaders understand the limitations and opportunities that result from the physical environment and make decisions accordingly.   1 2 3 4 5

32. Local government and community organizations carefully use fiscal resources and understand their fiduciary responsibilities.   1 2 3 4 5

33. Our community supports local business in planning for passing these businesses to new owners.   1 2 3 4 5

34. In our community, we see ourselves as part of a greater region and consider all the communities within that region in our planning.   1 2 3 4 5

Investment in the Community

35. Our community invests in its future by passing school bonds, hospital bonds, or library projects.   1 2 3 4 5

36. The community supports a community foundation or other types of local philanthropy.   1 2 3 4 5

37. Donations for projects come from all segments of the community.   1 2 3 4 5

38. We find resources for economic development projects. 1 2 3 4 5

39. Typical fundraising efforts result in many small gifts as well as large gifts.   1 2 3 4 5

40. The community recognizes and supports community volunteers.   1 2 3 4 5

41. Local businesses support the community through donations.   1 2 3 4 5

42. The community supports and maintains a sound and well-maintained infrastructure.   1 2 3 4 5

43. Our community shows a strong support for K-12 education plus life-long learning, job skills training and birth to 5 programs.   1 2 3 4 5

44. There's evidence in our community that the arts, music and our library are important parts of everyone's life. 1 2 3 4 5

**COMMUNITY
CAPACITY
QUESTIONNAIRE**

(continued)

Additional Resources

Your first stop for more information is the E^2 *Energizing Entrepreneurs* website, www.energizingentrepreneurs.org. Once there, click on "Building Capacity" to find resources that support the information in this chapter.

Your Field Guide to Community Building, by Vicki Luther and Mary Emery, includes an accompanying CD with stories and suggestions, tools and techniques from rural community builders nationwide. www.heartlandcenter.info/publications.htm

Community Organizing and Development by Herbert J. Rubin and Irene S. Rubin. 2001. 3rd edition. Allyn & Bacon. Massachusetts. The seminal work on increasing community capacity through empowerment and broad-based participation in decision making.

Organizing: A Guide for Grassroots Leaders, by Si Kahn. 1991. NASW Press. This publication is a how-to book for getting a group of folks behind a shared goal, with good information and wisdom about local politics and power.

CHAPTER 10
KEEPING SCORE

Why Keep Score?

There are many reasons why measuring progress is vital to the success of an entrepreneurship development effort. Keeping score or measuring results is probably the very best recruiting tool or motivational approach possible. Results get you more volunteers, more resources, more positive visibility. Measuring progress is also a way of building accountability into any project, whether the focus is on supporting entrepreneurs or on any type of community improvement. Keeping score will help you in a number of ways:

- Use progress reports to keep your volunteers energized and committed.
- Hold people, associations and organizations accountable for the work.
- Improve your effort by documenting successes and challenges.

Measuring the results or outcomes of your entrepreneurship development efforts is also critically important if you hope to influence policy in your community or state. If you can show how your efforts to energize entrepreneurs are having positive impacts on your community, you will have an easier time convincing decision makers of the merits of supporting your efforts through new policies, programs and resources. Plummer, Idaho, for example, used project reports to build a case for collaboration with tribal authorities in several areas of community and entrepreneurship development.

However, keeping score about the outcomes of entrepreneurship programs requires considering and measuring impacts a bit differently from more traditional economic development efforts. You need to think more broadly, and more long-term, about how your strategy to support entrepreneurs is changing the culture in your community, building new capacity among citizen leaders and creating businesses that bring jobs and wealth into your hometown.

Linesville, Pennsylvania, provides some insight about how this kind of thinking is somewhat different than traditional outcome measurement for economic development. Envision Linesville, Inc. is a collaboration among local business owners, government officials, the local chamber of commerce and community service organizations. Their mission is to increase citizen interest, involvement and activity in the greater Linesville area and to promote and encourage healthy lifestyles and lifelong learning. One of their major goals is to build on the existing tourism base, which includes avid hikers, bikers and sportsmen and women.

Within two years after their initial meetings the group reports these measurable outcomes:

- Established Envision Linesville, Inc. as a 501 (c) (3) nonprofit organization.
- Created a master plan to establish National U.S. Route 6 Visitor Center and Museum and developed a partnership with the U.S. Route Tourist Association.
- Created the Envision Linesville website to keep the community up-to-date on the organization's activities.

Building an Evaluation Strategy

Most evaluations these days incorporate a series of questions that frame the assumptions behind a program. A community group making decisions about what actions to take should be able to answer the following questions about their project plans:

- For whom?
- What assumptions?

- What process?
- What outcomes?
- What impact?

Called a **Program Logic Model**, this approach really offers a picture of how your program actually works. **We provide an example model at the end of the chapter**, but we'll also illustrate the model with an example here. If your community group decides to create a program that will identify local entrepreneurs and offer them some special types of assistance, the program logic model would look like this:

For Whom:	Local entrepreneurs Targeted youth groups
Assumptions:	Locally developed Driven by the needs of local entrepreneurs Combines education and support groups Emphasis on peer learning Requires collaboration among various service providers
Process:	One-stop shopping Easier access for the entrepreneurs Referrals from a variety of service providers Adaptation of many marketing and promotional techniques One-on-one and group activities

Outcomes:	Increased number of entrepreneurs identified
	Support group created and maintained
	Connections to funding and specialized
	    assistance programs
	High visibility for entrepreneurship creates
	    more community interest
	New business starts

Impact:	Local economy is diversified More dollars generated locally

The *program logic model* is a way to concentrate effort. This may sound very difficult, but remember that at the community level, this can be done through conversational, informal work sessions. Even if one or two people take responsibility for drafting the answers, a larger group can use the draft for discussion. Getting more folks involved also means that more ideas will be generated and nothing will be missed. The danger of one person designing a project is that sometimes the obvious can be overlooked, while a group discussion and review can provide a lot of oversight.

One mistake that a community group can make is to avoid any evaluation at all or to do nothing with the information. Either it's assumed that nobody in town is interested outside of the core group of volunteers or else the news opportunity of a progress report is simply overlooked. While there is a time and place for an "external' evaluation of a community effort, a powerful way to keep track of progress is to develop a local team of three or more volunteers who make it their special focus to measure progress and report on it. You might call this team of volunteers an evaluation subcommittee or a progress monitoring team. Their job is to take evaluation seriously and make the most of the opportunity to measure progress and report back to the community.

Sometimes high school or college students can be very effective as part of this team. A high school, community college or university class can be brought into the picture to help collect information about progress and construct new and interesting ways to report the results. Think about a high school math class that might do a summary of evaluations from participants in an entrepreneurship class. Making a presentation of the results at a city council meeting, with newspaper coverage and photos of the students, would be a great way to get people to support more efforts targeted at entrepreneurs.

Students in the Edcouch-Elsa, Texas, school district have proven that the talents and interests of young people can be put to work in reporting on community progress. There, a group of motivated young people established the Edcouch-Elsa Printing Center, which writes, produces and markets print and video products for their communities. They also established a national electronic network for alumni to make connections for possible future community and economic development in south Texas.

The Progress Monitoring Team

So, what does this team of volunteers do? They should answer some basic questions, always referring back to the goals set for working with entrepreneurs. Here's a review of the questions that form the work of the Progress Monitoring Team:

• WHERE ARE WE RIGHT NOW?

This question is all about establishing a beginning point or a baseline. For example, if you have a goal of "increasing the number of entrepreneurs identified in one year," then the question really means, "How many entrepreneurs have we identified in the last year? What's our starting point?" Remember, measuring progress is almost impossible if you don't know that starting point. It's like starting a diet when you don't know what you weigh—how can you tell how many pounds you've lost or gained? The team has to establish a baseline for whatever the goal might be.

• HOW WILL WE KNOW IF WE'VE MADE PROGRESS?

What will be an indicator of success? What evidence will we see if we've made progress? Indicators might be things like an increased number of participants at entrepreneur workshops or a higher percentage of telephone calls to the chamber that mention entrepreneurship issues. Indicators are simply the evidence that the group decides to watch for since those will be indications of progress.

• WHAT MEASURES WILL WE USE?

The team not only decides what evidence they will look for (indicators), they must also decide whether they will count something (numbers of participants, for example) or figure some percentages (a decrease in bankruptcy for small businesses, for example). In other words, in what quantitative way will they measure progress toward a goal? Of course, the team also must decide and act on ways to collect information in order to keep track of whatever measures they decide are most important.

It's most practical for the Progress Monitoring Team to decide on three to five indicators and just a few measures for each one of those. Any more indicators and measures makes for volunteer work that is way too complicated. Most importantly, the team has to guard against collecting too much data. Folks that volunteer for this task are usually people who are really interested and curious about information; it's all too easy for them to let the task become a vast and complicated data-gathering journey. The indicators and the measures that match them have to be significant, not just interesting! Once again, it's important for the team to focus.

Here's a look at a sample goal and the indicators, baseline, and measures a team might use to measure progress toward that goal. The Progress Monitoring Team should work with the goals established for your entrepreneurship development efforts and then brainstorm the types of indicators and measures that make sense for your community.

Goal:	Make entrepreneurship education the focus of our community's economic development efforts
Indicators:	Increased financial support for entrepreneurship classes Increased diversity among participants in entrepreneurship classes Attracting members to a new entrepreneurship support group
Baseline:	Current spending levels for entrepreneurship classes Age, gender and racial/ethnic background of people enrolled in the previous entrepreneurship classes Members, if any, in entrepreneurship support group
Measures:	Percent change in spending on entrepreneurship classes Percent change in participation in entrepreneurship classes by various demographics, e.g., participants under 30, persons of color Number of members in support group after one year

Balancing Stories and Statistics

Information about progress can take the form of either stories (qualitative) or numbers (quantitative). The Progress Monitoring Team should try to gather both kinds of information and use both to report to the community. Stories that feature an individual or a business can be inspiring proof that everyone's efforts are paying good dividends to the local community. However, reporting numbers of participants in entrepreneurship classes or a percentage of change over time in the number of entrepreneurs counseled or visited can be very compelling information at a budget meeting! Don't rely on just one type of information for a progress report. Broken Bow, Nebraska, has done a great job of getting media coverage that combines facts and human interest pieces to tell the whole story of each successful development effort.

Measuring Outcomes Over Time

Entrepreneurship development efforts take time. Entrepreneurship is a long-term economic development opportunity—not a short-term fix. However, it's important to show progress quickly, if possible, to keep the momentum and support for your efforts growing. You should consider both short- and long-term outcomes as you are developing measures of success. It's very important to match expectations regarding progress for your program with the appropriate time frame. For example, you may not want to use job creation measures to report progress in the first 6 or 12 months of your program. You should be focused on capacity-building measures like number of members recruited for your entrepreneurship steering committee, number of entrepreneurs visited by the steering committee, or number of newspaper articles written about entrepreneurs.

Once you move into the second year and beyond, you can begin to focus on measures that show a quantitative impact on the community, such as the number of new businesses started by entrepreneurs in your community. **When we talk about tools later in this chapter,** we'll introduce an **Outcome Measurement Tracking Tool** that can be very useful in matching measures and time frames.

Getting Information from Entrepreneurs

You really need two types of information from your entrepreneurs. You need tracking data on the business itself. Is the business growing? Are new jobs being created or existing jobs being saved? Is new capital coming into the business? These data usually come through the service providers that are working directly with entrepreneurs. While you don't want to overwhelm busy entrepreneurs with too many requests for data, it is important to be able to report back to funders and policy makers about the impact of all your efforts on entrepreneurs. We provide an **Outcome Tracking Tool at the end of the chapter** that you can adapt to meet these data collection needs in your community.

It's also extremely important to consistently get feedback from entrepreneurs—your customers! Listening to entrepreneurs can help you measure progress and, most importantly, improve your programs. A focus group of entrepreneurs held once a year can be an invaluable tool for measuring progress and for getting ideas on how to expand and improve efforts. This doesn't have to be a heavy burden for your volunteers either, since it's a great task to delegate to a high school or community college marketing class. And, it gets the students involved, too. **Later in this chapter,** we provide an **Entrepreneur Focus Group Questionnaire**—a tool that you can use and adapt for a focus group with entrepreneurs in your community.

Reporting Results to the Community

What should you do with the information the Progress Monitoring Team collects? Certainly, any funding department or agency gets a report, but we're concerned with getting the information out to the community. This is a significant way to build political support for entrepreneurship efforts, recruit volunteers and also to market a program to the users themselves! Cheney, Kansas, uses an annual town hall meeting to report progress and set future goals. If a team has collected some information that offers evidence of progress, here are some additional ways to get the word out to the wider community:

• NEWSPAPER ARTICLES

Feature stories of successful entrepreneurs, photos of participants in an entrepreneurship class, graphs of increased enrollment, use of services or any type of visual display of a measurement will make the paper.

• RADIO PROGRAMS

Taking calls on a local program can be an excellent opportunity to "brag" about your progress.

• CLUB AND CHURCH NEWSLETTERS

Feature success stories or even an abbreviated version of the newspaper article can help spread the word about your activities.

• SPECIAL MAILINGS

A brief cover letter and a one-page report to boards of directors or officers of service clubs and elected officials is a good way to keep them informed about your progress.

• WEB PAGE

Here's the place to show off all the photos, thank you letters and complete progress reports. Be sure your web address is printed on everything to encourage visitors.

• SPEAKERS' BUREAU

Develop a simple Power Point presentation or series of overheads and recruit two volunteers to make the rounds of the local service clubs with a 15-minute presentation on progress. Have a simple, one-page handout on the report and you're set to get folks talking about entrepreneurship ideas.

Evaluation Tools

We are providing the following four tools to help you measure the progress of your entrepreneurship development efforts:

Tool I.   **Program Logic Model**
Tool II.   **Outcome Measurement Tracking Tool**
Tool III.   **Entrepreneur Focus Group Questionnaire**
Tool IV.   **Entrepreneur and Small Business Community Metrics Tool**
Tool V.   **Paticipant Evaluation for Special Events**

You should adapt these tools for your community, to include specific measures that your Progress Monitoring Team decides are important. For example, if you are specifically targeting displaced workers with entrepreneurship education programs, you might want to conduct a focus group with displaced workers and workforce development board staff instead of (or in addition to) a focus group with entrepreneurs.

You can be creative in how you use these tools. Just remember—the most important thing is to make a commitment to keeping score and sharing your progress with the community!

TOOL I.

PROGRAM LOGIC MODEL

Tool I. Program Logic Model

Here's another example of a program logic model that could be used to guide and evaluate efforts to increase the support for entrepreneurs by local government.

For Whom:	Local entrepreneurs and small businesses less than one year old.
Assumptions:	Support of local government can make a positive difference in the success of new ventures in our community.
	The entrepreneurs themselves should be asked what local government support might be best.
	Having some supports and programs in place will encourage more entrepreneurs to identify themselves.

Process:	Interviews with any new business less than one year old.
	Focus group conversations with potential entrepreneurs about what might help.
	Research with state agencies and online resources about what other communities are doing to nurture entrepreneurs (model practice research).
Outcomes:	New local government initiative, program or service targeted at entrepreneurs.
	Increased visibility for entrepreneurs in our community.
	Exchange of information with other communities trying the same ideas.
Impact:	Local government services targeted at entrepreneurs in a systematic way.
	Percentage of community budget dedicated to entrepreneurship programs increased.
	Higher rate of new business starts and entrepreneurial activity.

TOOL I.

PROGRAM LOGIC MODEL
(continued)

Tool II. Outcome Measurement

The following tables may be helpful as your Progress Monitoring Team begins to discuss program goals and the indicators and measures used to track progress toward achieving those goals. We start with some common definitions and then offer examples of indicators that you might use to measure progress. This information should be used as a first step in identifying what is important to the entrepreneurial development efforts in your community and what type of indicators might be helpful in measuring those outcomes. We also organize these indicators into short-term and long-term so that you can encourage realistic expectations about your program's progress.

TOOL II.

OUTCOME MEASUREMENT

OUTCOME MEASUREMENT TRACKING TOOL—TERMS

Criteria	*Measures employed to support decision making or selection among various choices.*
Indicators	*Measures employed to track performance associated with specific actions or a program of work.*
Reach	*Relates to the scale of impact associated with an intervention.*
Impact	*Relates to the depth of outcome associated with an intervention.*
Capacity Building	*Relates to the ability of an initiative to engage in development activity.*

TOOL II.

OUTCOME MEASUREMENT

(continued)

Outcome Measurement Tracking Tool— Short-Term Outcomes (6 to 12 months)

Criteria	Indicators	Discussion
Enterprise Activity	• More Entrepreneurs Assisted • Increased Client Engagement • Increased Deal Flow • Better Deal Flow	Economic development is a long-term activity. Bottom line outcomes only happen over time. Measuring short-term success is problematic. However, there are short-term indicators that can track progress toward ultimate outcomes. An entrepreneurial focused approach centers on specific entrepreneurs and their ventures. Indicators of enterprise activity such as the number of entrepreneurs being assisted, the level of engagement with the entrepreneur, expanding deal flow (private investment into ventures), and the quality of the deal flow are all sound short-term indicators to track progress.
Capacity Building	• Focused & Strategic • Move from Reactive to Proactive • Adequate Capitalization • Community Engagement • Resource Articulation into More Rational Assistance System • Expanded Program Team	Chances are that any community, area or state seeking to build an entrepreneurial focused development program must start with what they have and evolve the program to greater sophistication, impact and reach—capacity building. We believe indicators within this evolutionary process measure whether the program is focused on entrepreneurs' needs and the strategic targeting of resources to entrepreneurship. Many development programs are reactive (e.g., responding to a new business lead or closing). Another measure of program success is when these programs move from being reactive to being proactive, thereby focusing resources on building a stronger entrepreneurial environment and meeting entrepreneurs' needs. Adequate funding of the program is essential and represents another measure. Expanding community engagement, understanding and, ultimately, support are essential for building a better program over time. One clear step is the articulation of available resources into a more rational, accessible, affordable and real-time assistance system for entrepreneurs. Finally, another measure is the development of a program team that is passionate and effective.

Outcome Measurement Tracking Tool—
Medium-Term Outcomes (1 to 3 years)

TOOL II.

**OUTCOME
MEASUREMENT**
(continued)

Criteria	Indicators	Discussion
Enterprise Success	• Increased Competitiveness • Increased Profitability • Successful Transfers to New Owners • Higher Survival Rates • Increased Startups • More Breakouts to New Markets and Growth	A big part of economic development is helping firms become more successful so that job creation, tax base expansion and other outcomes can be realized. In rural areas the keys to success begin with creating more competitive venture models that result in higher profitability, growth and reduced failure rates. Other indicators of enterprise success include higher rates of business transfer as aging owners are seeking exit strategies from their businesses. We also measure success with higher new business start-ups and entrepreneurial breakouts. Breakouts are successful businesses that create a more competitive model, enabling them to reach new markets and sustain growth.
Community Success	• Broader Career Options • Expanded Employment • Rise in Living Wage Jobs • Expanded Tax Base • Increased Give-Back to Communities	Economies exist to serve the needs of people within communities. Community success is a second tier of medium-term outcomes we are seeking. For example we typically are seeking job creation from our economic development efforts. But increasingly we are also seeking jobs with attractive career tracks. Educated and motivated rural youth will leave if good career options are not offered by their rural community. The term "quality jobs" has also emerged as a refined economic development goal. We want more than job numbers. We also want jobs that provide living wage incomes. Two other community outcomes include expanded tax base (thereby increasing the ability of a community to meet public needs) and increased give-back (the giving of time, talent and treasure to charitable causes).
Organizational Success	• Stronger Development Organization • More Sophisticated Development Agenda • Increased Volunteer Engagement • Larger Budget • Sharper Strategic Focus	In years 1 through 3 we are still creating capacity to engage in entrepreneurial focused economic development. A number of mid-term measures of organizational success include building a stronger development organization that can evolve a more sophisticated agenda. Such organizations inherently require more volunteer human talent, larger budgets for staff and programs, and an ever sharper strategic game plan.

TOOL II.

OUTCOME MEASUREMENT

(continued)

Outcome Measurement Tracking Tool— Long-Term Outcomes (3 years or larger)

Criteria	Indicators	Discussion
Creation of Rooted Wealth	• Increased Assets Per Household • More Equitable Distribution of Assets • Presence of Community Endowments and Philanthropic Giving	The long-term outcome of economic development investments should be the creation of rooted wealth. Measuring wealth is challenging, as appropriate and readily available secondary data are scarce. However some information is generally available, including asset property values (often by type such as residential, commercial, etc.) from state property tax databases. Information on assets per household can only be estimated using an indicator such as residential assessed value of property per household, for example. Income is also a limited indicator, as wealth per household is typically higher when higher income levels are sustained over time. Finally, with a little work, community endowments and philanthropic giving can be measured locally.
Sustainability	• Increased Diversity of Businesses in Economy • Increased Competitiveness of Businesses • Increased Local Ownership	Sustainability is an ecological concept suggesting environmental systems are robust and stable with a capacity to handle shocks (such as droughts). Sustainability can also be employed with economic and social systems. For example, an area economy with a wide range of business types is generally more sustainable when compared to a single industry town. Other indicators can include the competitiveness of the economy based on industry type and firm competitiveness, as well as the level of local ownership of firms.
Smart Growth	• Sustainable Development • Fits Scale of the Community • Minimized Disruptions	Smart growth suggests a bias. Actually smart growth refers to an emerging development approach that ensures growth is managed, intentional and beneficial to a broad segment of the community. Rapid or unplanned growth can be damaging to the social fabric of communities and fundamental quality of life.
Constituency	• Informed of Economic Development Strategies • Engaged in Developing and Implementing Strategies • Supportive with Time and Resources	Our democratic system, as well as market economic system, is based on an informed, engaged and supportive constituency. Active engagement of the residents of a community in economic development and community affairs is fundamental to the achievement of other long-term outcomes.

Entrepreneur Focus Group Questionnaire

The primary purpose of an entrepreneur focus group is to get some feedback from entrepreneurs on the programs and environment for entrepreneurship in your community. However, you'll also find that these groups provide an opportunity for entrepreneurs to network and share information with one another. Be sure to build in some flexible time so that this networking can occur. You can adapt the questions included here to more specifically reflect what's happening in your community. Ask for feedback on the specific programs you are offering.

TOOL III.

ENTREPRENEUR FOCUS GROUP QUESTIONNAIRE

ENTREPRENEUR FOCUS GROUP QUESTIONNAIRE

1. Take a few moments to tell us about yourself and your company. Why are you and your business located in this region? *(Go around the room and get answer from each participant.)*

2. What is the biggest challenge facing your business today?

3. Where do you turn when you have issues or problems with your business? Have you been satisfied with this support?

4. Have you ever used *(reference specific entrepreneurship development programs such as business counseling offered by the Small Business Development Center)* programs? Have you been satisfied with this support?

5. Please take a few moments to tell us a bit about your perceptions of economic development in your region. What are your key concerns in terms of future economic development in this region?

6. What are economic developers or local elected officials doing to help make your business successful? What more could they be doing?

7. Would you encourage your children to become entrepreneurs? In this community?

8. Do you feel that your community values and supports entrepreneurs like you? In what ways do you think the community could increase this support?

TOOL IV.

ENTREPRENEUR AND SMALL BUSINESS COMMUNITY METRICS TOOL

Tool IV. Entrepreneur and Small Business Community Metrics Tool

If you are going to collect quantitative data about your community's entrepreneurship programs, it is useful to have a common tracking tool that all of your partners use to record program participation and track the measures the Progress Monitoring Team has agreed are important. As part of the Georgia Entrepreneur Friendly Community program, communities are asked to collect data that can then be reported and aggregated at the state level. We provide this tool for you to use and adapt in your community.

ENTREPRENEUR AND SMALL BUSINESS COMMUNITY METRICS TOOL

COMMUNITY DATA

	To Date	This Period
# of Home Based Businesses		
# of Small Businesses		
SBA Loan Amounts		
Business Licenses Issued		
Building Permits Issued		

ENTREPRENEUR/SMALL BUSINESS (ESB) COMMITTEE ACTIVITY

	To Date	This Period
Committee Meetings		
Meeting Participants		
Community Presentations		
# of People Reached with Messages		
# of Media Pieces		
# of Entrepreneurs Identified		
# of Entrepreneurs Visited		

CLIENT CONTACTS

	To Date	This Period
# of Inquiries		
# of Existing Businesses Assisted		
# of Start-Ups Assisted		
# of Start-Up Kits Distributed		
# of Referrals Made:		
SBDC		
SBA		
Other		
Total		
SBDC Contacts from our Community		
SBDC Active Clients for our Community		
SBA Loans in Process/Submitted		
Other Community-Based Programs?		

TOOL IV.

ENTREPRENEUR AND SMALL BUSINESS COMMUNITY METRICS TOOL

(continued)

CLIENT DEMOGRAPHICS

	To Date	This Period
Female Contacts		
Male Contacts		
Ethnic Minority Contacts		
Nonprofit Entity Contacts		

IMPACT

	To Date	This Period
# of Jobs Created		
Full Time		
Part Time		
# of Jobs Saved		
# of Businesses Created		
Amount of Investment Assisted		
Amount of Contracts Assisted		
Business Turn Arounds		
Business Transfers		

TOOL V.

PARTICIPANT EVALUATION FOR SPECIAL EVENTS

Tool V. Participant Evaluation for Special Events

The results of participant evaluations of special events, such as workshops or presentations, can be useful for improving future programs. Here's a simple evaluation form that can be adapted to any workshop or presentation.

SAMPLE EVENT EVALUATION FORM

**"Everything You Would Like to Know about Entrepreneurs"
Workshop Evaluation**

1. Three things I really liked about this workshop:

2. Three changes I think would improve this workshop:

3. Something I learned today:

4. As a result of this workshop, I plan to…

5. Here's how I'd rate the following:

Effectiveness of the presenter

1	2	3	4	5
Not at all Effective				*Excellent*

Usefulness of the materials

1	2	3	4	5
Not at all useful				*Extremely useful*

Additional Resources

More information is available on the *E²* *Energizing Entrepreneurs* website, www.energizingentrepreneurs.org. Once there, click on "Keeping Score" to find resources that support the information in this chapter.

Make Success Measurable. Douglas K. Smith. 1999. John Wiley & Sons. Although this book is focused on teams in a business setting, the techniques for setting goals and measuring results are easily transferred to a community group or committee.

W.K. Kellogg Foundation Evaluation Handbook. 1998. This is an excellent resource guide to all types of evaluation and measurement, including the use of program logic models with a variety of examples used to illustrate keeping score. www.wkkf.org

Measuring Community Capacity Building: A Workbook-in-Progress for Rural Communities. 1996. Aspen Institute. A version of this workbook is available for free downloading at the Aspen Institute's website. It includes many examples of how to track and measure various aspects of community capacity that might seem impossible to quantify. www.aspeninstitute.org

CHAPTER 11
INFLUENCING POLICY TO SUPPORT ENTREPRENEURSHIP

Policy in Action

Let's begin with two stories to illustrate policy making to support entrepreneurship. Surry County, North Carolina, the real Mayberry RFD of Andy Griffith Show fame, had a thriving manufacturing and tobacco-based economy for many years. More recently, however, the factories closed and tobacco supports diminished, forcing community leaders to consider other economic development options. With support from the Appalachian Regional Commission and many private sector businesses, the county created a business plan competition for new entrepreneurs. The competition raised awareness about the potential role for entrepreneurs in creating new economic activity and prompted community leaders to talk about entrepreneurship strategies. The initial experiment is continuing with the support of the local economic development commission, the city and county chambers of commerce and the community college, helping to create an environment where entrepreneurship is recognized and celebrated.

In Georgia, Governor Sonny Perdue, a former entrepreneur, has focused attention at the state level on ways to support entrepreneurs. In 2004, he created by Executive Order the Georgia Entrepreneur and Small Business Coordinating Network. This multi-agency group is charged with coordinating the state's programs for entrepreneurs and small businesses. A new Office of Entrepreneur and Small Business Development within the state

Department of Economic Development facilitates the work of the Network. Listening to entrepreneurs and community leaders is one of the important activities of the Network. Through his leadership, the Governor is sending a signal that the state is serious about creating an environment that is supportive of entrepreneurship.

These two stories illustrate that policy intervention can occur at different levels. Our focus in this guide is helping rural community leaders think about, plan for and implement strategies to energize entrepreneurs. Part of this process requires becoming involved with policy in two ways—by working to create the most supportive environment for entrepreneurs at the community level and demonstrating the value of supporting entrepreneurs to state policy makers through your success. This chapter offers some useful insights for undertaking this adventure in policy making.

Why Engage Policy Makers?

Right now, disproportionate amounts of county, state and federal economic development resources are directed toward more traditional economic development strategies. These traditional approaches focus on attracting industries through incentives, supporting farm commodity programs and providing services to existing businesses. A 2002 survey of state expenditures on economic development conducted by the National Association of State Development Agencies found that $2.7 billion was allocated to both financial and non-financial assistance programs, but less than 1% of these investments went to programs that support entrepreneurship. The number could be higher in some states, as Erik Pages and Ken Poole found in a three-state study. Using a more specific definition of entrepreneurship development programs, they found that expenditures on entrepreneurship programs were much higher in Maine (29%), Nevada (40%) and Pennsylvania (64%).

Aside from money invested, more traditional economic development activities receive much greater public attention than do entrepreneurship programs. Ribbon cuttings for recruited industry abound, while small entrepreneurs create new ventures or add new employees without any public fanfare. And, in conversations with entrepreneurs around the country, this lack of recognition hurts!

Community leaders don't determine how state resources are allocated to economic development activities. County governments cannot influence national issues such as trade, fiscal and monetary policies. However, leaders at the community, county and even regional levels do play a fundamental role in creating a supportive and stimulating climate for entrepreneurs. The next section describes the elements of this supportive environment. By focusing on these elements and creating an environment that nurtures and grows entrepreneurs, your community efforts may become the model that influences policy makers in your statehouse.

Maximizing Impact – Community Level Policy

When we talk about community level policy, we're thinking about Webster's definition: a "high-level overall plan." Policy is more than just keeping taxes low and extending water and sewer to an industrial park. The plan that community leaders design and implement to support entrepreneurs (entrepreneurship policy) plays a central role in creating a stimulating and supportive environment for entrepreneurs.

In Chapter 7 we talked about the elements of an entrepreneurial environment. Communities can create this environment by making policy choices and decisions that produce a positive climate for entrepreneurship and by investing in infrastructure that supports entrepreneurs. While this environment has many features in common with places that boast a strong business climate, there are some important distinctions that can make all the difference to your entrepreneurs.

Climate for Entrepreneurship

Creating a supportive climate for entrepreneurship begins by recognizing the importance of the entrepreneurs who live and work in your community. Community leaders need to understand why these entrepreneurs are important to the economic development future of the community and communicate that understanding widely. This is particularly important for the growth entrepreneurs. These entrepreneurs have both the motivation and capacity to grow their ventures, bringing jobs, taxes and economic growth to your community. Understanding their needs and developing a climate that is supportive of them is an important first step in this process.

Creating a culture that supports and embraces entrepreneurship entails a number of different elements. Communities with an entrepreneurial culture regularly celebrate their entrepreneurs. They also recognize that these creative folks often may appear to be out of step with what is considered the rural "norm." Instead of isolating them because of their uniqueness, entrepreneurial communities accept entrepreneurs as a new and vital part of the community's social order. This isn't always an easy process. Writing for the Des Moines Register, columnist David Yepsen summed it up well. "Those of us who remain [in rural Iowa communities] often ridicule the failure of others, or are jealous of their success, which just drives away even more creative people. Nor do we welcome outsiders and those who don't look like us."

Community leaders must address the challenge of incorporating entrepreneurs into the social and political structure of the community. This means welcoming the "techie" who wants to develop a software business in an old tobacco barn, dealing with the suddenly successful local sporting goods retailer who has tapped the online market and continuing to support the manufacturing entrepreneur whose business has succumbed to competition.

So, what policies might community leaders consider to create this entrepreneurial support environment? Here are some ideas to get you started:

- A formal entrepreneur visitation program on the part of the chamber or economic developer sends a positive message that the community is interested in learning more about the needs and opportunities faced by its entrepreneurs.
- Creating an entrepreneur advisory group to the chamber or town council provides a pathway for entrepreneurs to share with community leaders and gives entrepreneurs an oppor-

tunity to get involved in leadership roles.

- A powerful way of creating a cultural shift toward entrepreneurship is to engage youth in the community. Working with the local school board to institute an entrepreneurship education program in K-12 classrooms and developing a youth leadership program are two ways of tapping into the potential that youth have to create a different economic future for themselves and their communities.

- Establishing award programs to honor an entrepreneur of the year or an entrepreneur who gives back to youth or the comeback entrepreneur of the year are relatively simple but effective ways of honoring the entrepreneurs in your midst and providing role models to others in your community with entrepreneurial aspirations.

- A branding campaign for your community's entrepreneurs can draw attention to their importance to your economy and create a sense of identity among entrepreneurs in your community. Plaques or stickers can identify a business as owned by "A Mayberry Entrepreneur."

The entrepreneurial climate you are working to create differs from a business climate because entrepreneurship is fundamentally about developing human resources—the entrepreneurs—and not just developing businesses. Community leaders must work to create an environment where entrepreneurs want to live, play and plant their businesses. This approach requires thinking a bit differently about community infrastructure to support entrepreneurs. In effect, leaders must keep an "entrepreneurial impact statement" in their heads. When considering new ideas or initiatives, they must ask themselves "what does it mean for local entrepreneurs?" Much like an environmental impact statement, this concept ensures that leaders "do no harm" to their local entrepreneurial climate.

Community Infrastructure

Economic development infrastructure has traditionally been about physical infrastructure—industrial parks and sites, water and sewer, access to interstates, rail and air transportation. We were less concerned about support services for business since branch plants usually came equipped with management and financial support from the headquarters location. Local financial institutions were called upon to finance the mortgages of relocating workers rather than the expansion needs of branch plants.

Entrepreneurs, however, have an expanded set of infrastructure needs. In terms of physical infrastructure, community leaders need to consider how well connected their community is to regional, national and even international markets and services. A rural entrepreneur may be able to start a company digitizing medical records, but only if he has reliable access to high speed, broadband Internet service. Entrepreneurs also need access to different types of space as their business grows—something different from the industrial park. For example, in Siler City, North Carolina, an artisan can expand her business from her home to an arts incubator located in a renovated, historic Main Street building.

Entrepreneurs also need support infrastructure—the collection of service providers who can help with finance, technical assistance, mentoring and networking. Entrepreneurial communities like Littleton, Colorado, place a premium on meeting the information needs of entrepreneurs who are starting and growing their ventures. Other communities make financing more accessible to entrepreneurs through micro loan programs. Community leaders can make a commitment to invest in the types of support infrastructure needed in the community just as they have invested in roads and industrial parks in the past. Many rural communities will lack the scale to have such resources close to home. Links to regional, national, and international expertise are essential to filling the service gaps that exist close to home.

A supportive entrepreneurial environment also includes quality of life infrastructure. Remember, entrepreneurship is about the people. Entrepreneurs choose to locate their businesses in places where they wish to live. Communities that invest in quality of life infrastructure (good schools, fine recreation programs and facilities, cultural venues like museums and theatres, quality community facilities such as renovated downtown markets and a preserved natural environment) are more likely to attract entrepreneurs from outside the community and keep those who are home-grown.

How can community leaders develop infrastructure policies to support entrepreneurs? Here are some ideas:

- Community policies toward home-based businesses should make it easy for start-up entrepreneurs to begin in their basements, garages or spare bedrooms.
- You can help entrepreneurs through the regulatory maze by creating a one-stop shop for new entrepreneurs at your chamber or local government office. Something as simple as a guide that details "How to start a local business" will be greatly appreciated by new business owners. Start by talking to entrepreneurs, those just getting started and those in business for some time. Find out where they got information on doing business in your community. Identify the stumbling blocks and take steps to ease the red tape for your entrepreneurs.
- Provide office space in your community for regional service providers and invite them to hold office hours once a week or twice a month. This simple move can expand access to services for your community's entrepreneurs.
- Contact service providers in your community (lawyers, accountants, marketing professionals) and ask them to volunteer a few hours per month to work with startup or aspiring entrepreneurs—a Community Entrepreneurial Support Team (CEST). Give these "civic entrepreneurs" recognition in the community and honor their efforts.
- Form an Entrepreneurial Capital Access committee, including local bankers, service providers and entrepreneurs, to explore gaps in financing for local entrepreneurs. Take steps to create a revolving loan fund, microenterprise fund or local angel network as needs are identified.

Creating an entrepreneurial environment is more complex than building an industrial park or a connector to the Interstate. Throughout this book, we've featured communities like Fairfield, Iowa, that are working hard to build an environment that is a magnet for entrepreneurs. These stories can help guide you as you develop the entrepreneurship policy that is right for your community. Once you've done that, what role can you play in beginning to transform economic development policy in your state?

Leveraging Community Work – State Level Policy

While we are convinced that the real work of creating entrepreneurship development policy must begin at the community level, state leaders are responsible for developing and implementing economic development policy at the state level. These policies, in turn, can be supportive of entrepreneurship development efforts at the community level. All too often, however, entrepreneurship development programs take a back seat to recruitment and retention strategies.

As community leaders, you have a role to play in state policy by demonstrating the potential of entrepreneurship development in your community. This requires careful documentation of your program and the outcomes of your investments. The information on program evaluation in Chapter 10 is very important to this process. Armed with this information, community leaders can share their stories with state legislators, agency representatives from the state department of commerce and newspaper reporters. You can also share the stories of your community's entrepreneurs. Nothing is as powerful as hearing a passionate entrepreneur share her story. Invite entrepreneurs to lunch with your local legislator. Organize an entrepreneurs' roundtable in your region and invite the press. By sharing your experience with entrepreneurship development with a wider audience, you can contribute to changing the attitude toward entrepreneurship in your state.

The first step in creating a dialogue with state policy makers is identifying the "go to" staff. You should get to know the key staff people for the state legislator from your region and for the legislators who chair key committees—economic development, small business, agriculture, education. Add these staffers to your mailing list and send them reports and special event announcements. You should also get to know key staff within your state departments of commerce or economic development, education and agriculture. Keep them informed of your progress and successes. Provide them with an opportunity to bask in the reflected glories of the accomplishments in your community!

For those of you who are state elected officials, it is useful to consider the following initial steps that state government might take to support entrepreneurship:

- **Create a focus on entrepreneurship as a development strategy.** States such as Georgia, West Virginia and Minnesota hold entrepreneurship summits to focus on entrepreneurs. North Carolina's Rural Economic Development Center has created the Institute for Rural Entrepreneurship as a focal point for entrepreneurship policy and programs in the state. Wisconsin and Georgia have created entrepreneurship divisions within their state development agencies to pay particular attention to entrepreneurship policy. Other states such as Arkansas engaged in assessments of the environment for entrepreneurship as a means of stimulating discussion and action.

- **Support innovative entrepreneurship projects at the community level.** When it comes to entrepreneurship policy, there is no "one-size fits all" strategy. Each community can and should develop a unique, locally tailored approach. A number of states have made investments in such community-based entrepreneurship projects. These projects can serve as a demonstration to the state and other communities about the outcomes of entrepreneurship programs. In a time of limited public sector resources, the state should consider ways that categorical programs can be used to support these innovative programs. For example, both Kansas and North Carolina are using Community Development Block Grants to support entrepreneurship projects in communities and regions of the state. In Nebraska, social service funds are used to support micro lending and self-employment strategies. Maine has altered its workforce programs to permit self-employment as an option for retraining.

- **Encourage service provider networks.** States often have many resources that provide technical and financial assistance to entrepreneurs. However, the services often fail to meet the needs of entrepreneurs because they are not integrated and do not operate as a system. Too many times entrepreneurs tell us that they "don't know where to go for help" or "I was referred from one place to another until I just gave up." Although many of these resources are not state supported, state policy makers have some tools at their disposal to try to encourage a more systemic approach. State government could convene the service providers so that they can begin to share information about their services and develop the comfort level with each other needed to foster cooperation. For state-supported service providers, the state could change performance standards to encourage, or even require, collaboration among service providers.

These three steps can begin the process of moving the state toward a more balanced economic development policy—one that recognizes the importance of entrepreneurs and supports strategies to energize entrepreneurs.

Just as there is no one strategy for supporting entrepreneurs, there is no single strategy for state policy makers to follow. However, two examples help to illustrate different paths to creating more supportive state policy environments for entrepreneurship.

Kansas Economic Growth Act of 2004

Through the leadership of a bipartisan group of state elected officials, Kansas launched a new era of economic development in 2004. The Kansas Economic Growth Act (KEGA) represents a departure from more traditional policies because of its strong focus on entrepreneurship support. The entrepreneurship component of this legislation includes creation of several key supports:

- The Kansas Center for Entrepreneurship (KCE) whose role is to create an integrated system of support among existing entrepreneurial support providers, including a one-stop resource clearinghouse with both a call center and website.
- The Kansas Community Entrepreneurship Fund (KCEF), managed by the KCE Board, to make grants to local and regional economic development organizations that will, in turn, provide seed capital to entrepreneurs. The state made an initial investment in KCEF as well as providing tax cred-

its to individuals and corporations that invest in the fund.

- The Angel Investor Network Tax Credit Program to provide 50% tax credits to qualified investors who bring both capital and their expertise to start-ups in the state.
- Additional operating funds to support the ongoing efforts of the five Enterprise Facilitation projects currently operating in 25 economically distressed rural counties throughout the state.
- The Agri-Tourism Initiative to assist rural communities and agri-entrepreneurs as they respond to opportunities in the tourism industry.

The KEGA initiative is a state policy response to issues raised at regional planning sessions held throughout the state in 2003. More than 1500 community and business leaders provided feedback on ways to stimulate economic activity in their regions.

What can other states learn from Kansas? There are three main lessons.

- Collaborate and leverage resources across support providers, both public and private.
- Be creative in financing entrepreneurship initiatives by using tax credits and encouraging private investment.
- Let state policies be driven by the needs in the regions and communities—take a "bottom up" approach to policy development.

North Carolina's Institute for Rural Entrepreneurship

In 2003, North Carolina's Rural Economic Development Center (REDC) asked a relatively straightforward question— What is the environment for entrepreneurship in rural North Carolina? The REDC is a nonprofit organization established by the state legislature in 1987 with a mission to serve the state's 85 rural counties.

Using the REDC's well-tested model of conducting research to inform state policy, the REDC partnered with the RUPRI Center for Rural Entrepreneurship to answer this question. Through a series of focus groups with entrepreneurs and service providers all across rural North Carolina and discussions with state and regional policy makers, the REDC identified some very specific needs and opportunities for rural entrepreneurship in the state. In the fall of 2003, the REDC announced the creation of its Institute for Rural Entrepreneurship with a 10-point agenda:

- Coordinate a new statewide alliance of business service providers.
- Serve as the leading information source on rural entrepreneurship in the state, through data and outreach.
- Improve access to business information and assistance.
- Promote high-quality entrepreneurship education and training opportunities.
- Expand business finance services in rural communities.
- Expand use of information technology in rural communities.
- Expand opportunities for agricultural entrepreneurs.
- Create self-employment opportunities for laid-off workers.
- Advocate for policies that benefit rural entrepreneurs.
- Demonstrate promising entrepreneurship models through grants to communities.

What can other states learn from North Carolina? There are four key lessons:

- Use solid applied research to guide the creation of state policy. It is easier to build support for policy when it is driven by real, identified needs among entrepreneurs in the state.
- Promote broad collaboration across many partners, public, private and nonprofit. There is plenty of work for everyone and coordinating efforts can lead to the more effective use of resources.
- Tap traditional sources of funds to support less traditional programs. For example, the community demonstration project grants were funded using Community Development Block Grant funds.
- Build capacity in rural communities to support entrepreneurship. While there are many service providers throughout rural North Carolina that can assist entrepreneurs, there are few organizations focused on expanding the capacity of communities to build supportive environments for entrepreneurship. The Institute serves to fill this gap.

Additional Resources

For more information visit the *E²* *Energizing Entrepreneurs* website, www.energizingentrepreneurs.org. Click on "Policy" to find resources that support the information in this chapter.

While much has been written about the policy-making process, we think the following pieces are most appropriate for those of you working at the community level:

Entrepreneurship: A Candidate's Guide by the National Commission on Entrepreneurship.
http://www.entreworks.net/library/reports/4249NCOEGUIDE.pdf

Key Issue Areas for Rural Public Policy by the Association for Enterprise Opportunity's Rural Committee. www.ruraleship.org

Strategies for Sustainable Entrepreneurship by the Central Appalachian Network. www.rural.eship.org

CHAPTER 12
SUSTAINING YOUR COMMUNITY, YOUR EFFORTS AND YOURSELF

This guidebook has offered a great deal of information, new ideas and step-by-step methods to help your community focus on entrepreneurship as a strategy for improving and sustaining a high quality of life into the future. But, how do you keep it all going? How do you keep new ideas and innovations as a central part of your work? And how do you keep yourself focused and motivated?

Your own personal motivation may turn out to be the key ingredient as you chart a new course for your rural community's future. It may come down to your own energy level, your own ideas and your abilities to communicate and involve others. Your level of commitment may make the difference between a good start that diminishes and then disappears, versus a good start that evolves into a truly transformed community journey.

Where Do New Ideas Originate?

A long-held tenant of adult education and the study of how change happens in a culture involve the recognition that much "learning" is really the discovery of what we already know in one part of life that can be applied to another. So when a community developer returns home from a conference with new ideas, one way to communicate the new ideas is to couch them in what local folks already know. Sometimes the best learning is accomplished by cross-referencing or applying something that is already familiar. New, fresh ideas from one realm can be transferred to another. For example, a farmer might not think he knows much about transportation systems and delivery of goods until he is reminded that he pays an annual fuel bill, maintains equipment, and factors in depreciation when he does his taxes. There's a lot of basic knowledge and experience that can be transferred.

On the other hand, it's important to realize that focusing on entrepreneurship as a development strategy does, in fact, require a fresh approach and a new way of thinking. This approach holds a community responsible for creating self-reliance and locating resources inside the community. In many cases, after years of dependence on outside agencies and programs, we're asking local folks to grow their own businesses, to really take charge of the local economy, and to build the skills necessary to create a future for their community. It's a new opportunity for people to rediscover an old idea that's come around again. Energizing local entrepreneurs can be seen as a return to the way we built communities during the frontier or settlement era. No new ideas under the sun, right? Sometimes it's the application or interpretation of the old that creates innovation.

How Do We Stay on Task?

"Eyes on the Prize" said the leaders of the Civil Rights Movement in the 1960s. They meant that leaders really had to hold a focus on the end goal in order to stay on target, keep their thinking strategic and refuse to let obstacles deter their purpose. In a similar way, community developers have to keep their focus, too. This is one of the best uses for a Vision Statement or even a list of short- and long-term goals. These statements, far from being a staging activity or just an exercise, provide a valuable filter for all the variables that can get in the way of a community project. Keep asking: Will this (activity or behavior or strategy) get us closer to where our community needs to be or farther away from it?

Investigate your own local history and look for models of community success. Who were the people who accomplished changes? What was their focus? Was there a person who held steadfast to a goal? Someone who came to every single village board meeting to lobby for a new community center? Was there a group that championed a cause and kept at it until it was achieved? That's the kind of model we need to keep on task and to maintain progress. That's how things get done.

How Do We Keep Motivated?

Often, the type of community work we are doing is almost invisible. If we are truly building capacity, then others are doing the up front work while we're laying the groundwork and coaching from behind the scenes. There is, however, a cost to being behind the scenes all the time. Sometimes our organizations or programs don't get the credit for what happens. In one sense that's okay, but being invisible can put our budgets at risk. The community needs to know that we are doing our job, moving forward and having an impact.

So there's a fine line of balance between accepting recognition and creating capacity in others. When we're asking folks to change the way they think about their community and set off on a new pathway to the future, we're bound to encounter some negative attitudes. It can certainly be discouraging to hear more criticism than praise for our accomplishments.

That's why everyone who does this work needs support. And we need the kind of support that goes beyond getting quoted in the paper or receiving a plaque from the Mayor. We also need the kind of support that means folks say "hello" and "good job" when we're at the gas pump or grocery store.

One way to keep motivation high is to construct your own support group. Maybe you should have a few trusted allies that you have breakfast with once a week. Or try scheduling a regular, private report to the mayor. It might mean offering a short program to a service club every six months, teaching a high school class, or mentoring a club of young entrepreneurs. You really have to do some thinking about what your own support needs are and then be proactive about getting those needs met.

What's most important is this element of actively constructing an environment that's supportive for you. Don't just wait to see if anyone will ask you to join or offer you some rewarding contact—make it happen for yourself.

Never Stop Learning

Learning is a motivational tool in itself. And the opportunities are endless. You can read books, you can research on the Internet, but you can also learn from other people—at conferences and training sessions—and from people in your own hometown. Use the additional resources mentioned in this publication as a place to begin exploring what others are doing in the area of community entrepreneurship. Do some serious thinking about your own skills, strengths and weaknesses. What do you really need to learn or improve upon? Budget in some time to give yourself a chance to learn. It not only opens up new pathways; it also validates our ideas and opinions in ways that are encouraging and motivating.

The Incredible Value of Networking

Beyond the local contacts who can offer you support and inspiration, you should look at the larger picture and find ways to connect with others in a wider arena. Attending conferences and training opportunities is only one way to meet others engaged in this work. Telecommunications and the Internet have literally put the world at our desktop. Finding a peer network is just a matter of finding the time to network, but it is so important. Don't underestimate the value of getting an email from another community developer facing the same trials and tribulations that you do! Your peers can offer you empathy and problem-solving conversation and maybe even suggestions on where else to look for help and advice.

Networking also offers an amazing array of solutions to common community problems. And the ability to offer examples from similar communities can be a powerful persuasion tool when you are making a case. Stories like the ones included in this guide are effective teaching and learning tools for elected officials, board members, voters—all the folks you'll need to engage in new strategies to energize entrepreneurs.

So how do you get started in this networking process? Follow up by checking in on the various websites cited in this guide. Do some Internet research on the many places and organizations mentioned in the preceding chapters. Go ahead and contact some of these folks and ask them to tell you their stories.

Join a statewide or national association, such as the National Rural Economic Developers Association or the International Community Development Society, and seek out interest groups that are focused on entrepreneurship.

Read, talk, listen—keep the information flowing as a way to keep your own interest high.

Taking Care of Yourself and Your Community

Lastly, remember that trying to accomplish big things for a community is an exhausting and demanding vocation. It's not just a job. It really is a calling—one that takes a great amount of energy but also offers amazing rewards. In order to do your best, you have to take good care of yourself in physical, mental and spiritual ways.

It's not our purpose here to suggest that everyone should reserve a time to meditate, attend a religious service or even join a health club. It does, however, make a huge difference in the effectiveness of your work if you figure out a way to step back occasionally and take a look at the big, big picture.

It's often said that community development is a messy business. So is democracy. Helping your community energize entrepreneurs and increase capacity to improve and sustain quality of life for the long-term—while involving as many citizens as possible—is exactly what democracy is all about. Communities where these types of activities occur regularly are the true strength of our country and important to all of us. Your work and your community are important to all of us. As you chart a new course for your community, please, take care!